African Spurred Tortoise

African Spurred Tortoise Pets

African Spurred Tortoise book for care, housing, keeping, diet and health.

By

Daniel Grimson

Published by: Zoodoo Publishing

Table of Contents

Introduction

I want to thank you and congratulate you for buying the book 'African Spurred Tortoise as a pet'. This book will help you to understand everything you need to know about domesticating an African Spurred Tortoise or Sulcata. You will learn all the aspects related to keeping the animal successfully at home. You will be able to understand the pros and cons, behaviour, basic care, breeding, keeping, housing, diet and health issues related to the animal.

If you wish to own a Sulcata or even if you already own one, it is important to understand the basic characteristics of the animal. You should know what you can expect from the animal and what you can't. This will help you to tweak the way you behave with the Sulcata in the household, which in turn will help to build a strong bond between the pet and you.

Domestication of an animal has its unique challenges and issues. If you are not ready for these challenges, then you are not ready to domesticate the animal. It is important that you understand that owning any pet will have its advantages and disadvantages.

A pet is like a family member. You will be more like a parent than like a master to the pet. You will be amazed to see how much love and affection your Sulcata will give through his ways and actions. But, for that to happen you have to make sure that the animal is taken care of. The animal should be loved in your household. If your family is not welcoming enough for the pet, the animal will lose its sense of being very quickly.

The diet of the Sulcata will have a direct effect on the way he feels and functions. As the owner of the pet, it will be your responsibility that the pet is fed the right food in the right amounts and at the right times. You will also have to make sure that the pet is safe and secure at all times. It is important that you learn about the common health issues that the Sulcata is likely to suffer from. This will help you to avoid these health conditions and keep the Sulcata safe.

If the African Spurred Tortoise does not feel wanted and loved in your home, you will see a decline not just in its behaviour but also its health. This is the last thing that you should do to an animal. An animal deserves as much love and protection as a human being. You should be able to provide the pet a safe and sound home. Your family should be caring towards the pet. You have to be like a parent to the Sulcata. This is the basic requirement when planning to bring an animal home.

If you have already bought a Sulcata, even then you need to understand your pet so that you take care of him in a better way. You should see whether with all its pros and cons, the animal fits well into your household. Domesticating and taming a pet is not only fun. There is a lot of hard work that goes into it.

Once you form a relationship with the Sulcata, it gets better and easier for you as the owner. The pet will be intelligent and adorable. He will also value the bond as much as you do. This will be good for the pet and also for you as the pet owner in the long run. It is important that you are ready to commit before you decide to domesticate the animal. If you are a prospective buyer, then understanding of these points will help you to make a wise decision.

When you bring a pet home, it becomes your responsibility to raise the pet in the best way possible. You have to provide physically, mentally, emotionally and financially for the pet. All these points are not being discussed to frighten or scare you. In fact, these points are being discussed to make you understand that you have to know the right ways to domesticate a pet. If the animal establishes a trust factor with you, he will always remain loyal to you. This is a great quality to have in a domesticated animal.

The pet will actually surprise you with their intelligence. This makes the pet all the more endearing. His unique ways and antics will leave you and the entire family in splits. If you have had a bad day, your pet will surely help you to release all the tension and enjoy life. If you are looking for a pet that is affectionate, lovable and fun, then the Sulcata is the ideal choice for you as they won't disappoint you.

If you are looking forward to raising a Sulcata as a pet, there are many things that you need to understand before you can domesticate the animal. You need to make sure that you are ready in terms of the right preparation. There are certain unique characteristics of the animal that make him adorable, but these traits can also be very confusing for many people. You can't domesticate the animal with all the confusions in your head.

There are still many doubts regarding their domestication methods and techniques. There are many things that the prospective owners don't understand about the animal. They find themselves getting confused as to what should be done and what should be avoided. If you are still contemplating whether you wish to buy a Sulcata or not, then it is important that you understand all about the maintenance of the pet, so that you can make the right choice for yourself. This book will help you make that decision.

This book is meant to equip you with all the knowledge that you need to have before buying the Sulcata and bringing it home. This book will help you understand the basic behaviour and antics of the animal. You will also learn various tips and tricks. These tips and tricks will be a quick guide when you are looking for different ways to have fun with your pet.

You will learn many ways to take care of your Sulcata. This book will try to address every question that you might have when looking at raising the animal. You will be able to understand the pet and give it the care that it requires.

You can expect to learn the pet's basic behaviour, nursery needs, eating habits, shelter requirements, breeding, grooming and training techniques among other important things. In short, the book will help you to be a better owner by learning everything about the animal. This will help you form an everlasting bond with the pet.

Chapter 1: About the African Spurred Tortoise

The African Spurred Tortoise is one of the most popular tortoises today. The Geochelone Sulcata, or African Spurred Tortoise, is known for its animated personality as well as its toughness. It does well even in captivity. The tortoise is given its name because of a very significant characteristic. The tortoise is primarily found in the Sahara desert of Africa. The front legs of the African Spurred Tortoise have pointed, large scales.

It should be noted here that African Spurred Tortoise is often confused with another popular tortoise called the Spur Thighed Tortoise. These two types of tortoises have front legs with enlarged scales and also similar names, leading to the confusion.

To avoid his confusion, African Spurred Tortoise is also referred to as the Sulk tortoise owing to its scientific name of Geochelone Sulcata.

1. Taxonomy and etymology

The name Sulcata is derived from a latin word, sulcus. The word sulcus means furrow. These furrows refer to the furrows on the Sulcatas.

Kingdom- Animalia
Phylum- Chordata
Class- Reptilia
Order- Testudines
Suborder- Cryptodira
Family- Testudinidae
Genus- Centrochelys
Species- C. Sulcata

2. What does the African Spurred Tortoise look like?

This is a very important question that any pet enthusiast will have. It is important to understand how the animal looks. This will also help you to decide whether this is what you are looking for in a pet animal. This section will help you to understand this.

It is important to note here that the African Spurred Tortoise is third largest tortoise in the world, and it is the largest tortoise in Africa.

The looks of the pet are in accordance with its natural habitat. The animal is found mainly in desert regions in Africa.

This allows the African Spurred Tortoise to camouflage with its sandy colour. This keeps him safe from potential threats in the desert areas.

If you look at the skin of the African Spurred Tortoise closely, you will notice that the skin is yellow brown to golden in colour. The covering shell is hard and is brown in colour.

The shell of the African Spurred Tortoise is oval in shape. There are grooves at the back brims and front brims. These grooves are big enough to be noticeable.

There are growth rings on the African Spurred Tortoise that become clearly marked as the African Spurred Tortoise ages. These growth rings are conspicuous in presence.

If you notice the forelimbs of the African Spurred Tortoise, scales conceal the anterior surface. These are coinciding and are very large in shape and size.

If you notice the thighs of the Sulcata, the posterior surface will allow two to three conical spurs. These spurs are so significant to the looks of the African Spurred Tortoise that the animal got its name after these spurs.

3. Size of the African Spurred Tortoise

The C. Sulcata or the African Spurred Tortoise is the largest tortoise species in the mainland tortoises.

It is also the third largest tortoise species in the entire world. The Galapagos Tortoise and Aldabra Giant Tortoise are larger than the African Spurred Tortoise.

The adult African Spurred Tortoise reaches a length of 33 inches or 83 cm. The adult African Spurred Tortoise can weigh 105 kg or 231 pounds.

The hatching of the African Spurred Tortoise is only 2 to 3 inches. But, the growth rate of the African Spurred Tortoise is very high and they grow quickly.

The Sulcata can grow from the hatchling of 2 to 3 inches to about 7 to 10 inches in just the first few years.

4. Understanding the geography and habitat

It is important to understand the geography and habitat range of the African Spurred Tortoise. This will help you to understand the animal better, which in turn will help you provide better care for the animal in captivity.

The main home of the African Spurred Tortoise is believed to be a 250 mile area which is located 13 degrees N latitude to North of Ethiopia, Eritrea.

The area is basically a narrow strip of land from the North Africa between the savannah forest and the Sahara desert. This is the Sudan region and it lies to the south of the Sahara Desert.

It is important to note here that this area is not the typical Sahara desert, and neither is it the typical savannah. It is a transition area of zone. This zone is also called the Sahel. This special bio zone has grass, dwarfed trees and short sized shrubs.

It is known that the Sahel zone will behave like the savannah for a few years and will show signs of the Sahara desert for some years. This is because of the special bio zone that it lies in. This is very interesting and effects all life forms thriving there.

The area can expect to receive rain anywhere between five to twenty inches in a year. This rain falls mostly in the months of July to November, which is the typical monsoon season in the area.

The weather is not the only unique element of the Sahel region. The soil patterns also exhibit uniqueness.

The soil in the Sahel is more fertile than the soil of the Sahara desert. But, it should be noted here that the Sahel soil is not as fertile as the Sudan soil. So, while Sahel receives good amounts of rain in the monsoon region, the vegetation remains stunted.

The African Spurred Tortoises dig burrows. They do this mainly in the monsoon season from July to November. It is basically preparation to face the dry spell in the summers.

These burrows are useful throughout the year. The mid-day temperatures in the Sahel region are very high. The tortoises use the burrows to save themselves from these high temperatures.

An African Spurred Tortoise is very skilled in making burrows. A typical burrow constructed by the Sulcata can have a vertical depth of 20 feet and horizontal length of over 30 feet.

The burrow is very deep so that the tortoise can feel safe and also because the temperature will be relatively stable. The temperature outside can fluctuate a lot throughout the day. The depth of the burrows also allows for humidity levels over fifty per cent.

As stated earlier an African Spurred Tortoise is very skilled in making burrows. The burrows are so skilfully divided into tunnels and chambers.

The different chambers are well connected by different tunnels. This gives the burrow a definite structure.

The African Spurred Tortoise is not the only animal that uses its burrows. Different chambers are known to be used by other animals that come there to look for refuge from the severe weather conditions.

It should be noted here that most of these animals that use the chambers of the burrows of the African Spurred Tortoise are later used as a source of food by the animal. This is particularly done in the lean period.

This shows a very important trait of the African Spurred Tortoise. Most tortoises, including the African Spurred Tortoises are known as opportunistic feeders. This trait is mostly exhibited in the wild. They will feed on what is available.

When the dry spell is at its peak, the Sulcatas prefer to remain mostly inactive. They prefer to stay in the burrows that they had constructed. A tortoise will seldom be visible outside its burrow at such times.

Rainy season brings about a change in the inactive African Spurred Tortoises. The tortoises begin to forage and also replace the lost reserves so that they are ready for reproduction.

It is this season when the tortoises breed and lay their eggs. The Sulcatas don't have a season exclusively for breeding.

The population of the male African Spurred Tortoises is lower. The breeding can occur throughout the year if the male African Spurred Tortoise has an encounter with the female African Spurred Tortoise, but that does not happen often.

During the dry spell, the tortoises are really inactive so chance encounters don't happen. At the beginning and also towards the rainy season in the region, the Sulcatas are very active so there is a probability of a male encountering a female Sulacata.

The breeding process can be expected between November to May. The nesting process by the female tortoise is done generally at the base of the bushes. The female can lay up to 24 eggs. It is known that the eggs that are deposited are usually less than 24.

The size of the eggs that the female tortoise lays and the number of tortoise eggs that are deposited have a correlation. A large clutch size will lead to smaller eggs. On the other hand, a small clutch size will result in larger sized eggs.

These eggs will lead to hatchlings. It is known that it usually takes 100 to over 200 days for the hatchlings to appear. The exact time will depend on the time when the eggs were deposited.

There are many factors that will affect the growth of the hatchlings. All these and more will be discussed in the subsequent chapters.

It is important to learn here that the young Sulcatas are quite large. They don't spend time in the nest and will be very eager to leave. The young ones will show tremendous growth in the first two years.

The resources available to the hatchlings also effect the growth of the young ones. A scarcity of the resources can have a hard effect on their growth process.

It is also known that the young ones can gain weight in excess of two pounds after the very first year. These young tortoises attain about seven pounds after the second year.

5. Opportunistic feeders

Most tortoises, including the African Spurred Tortoises, are known as opportunistic feeders. This trait is mostly exhibited in the wild. They will feed on what is available.

Rainy season in the Sahel region leads to abundant vegetation. The Sulcata happily feeds on this vegetation, including broad leaf weed, grass, fruits and leaves of various bushes and trees.

After the rainy season is over, the food pattern of the Sulcata changes a bit. The dry season that follows leads to dried leaves and plants. The tortoise feeds on these organic dried plants.

There are spells of dry weather where the plants show little to no growth. But the tortoise can adapt even to that weather. They consume carrion, animal faeces, tree barks and branches during such dry spell.

The tortoise allows many other animals to use the various chambers in the burrow constructed by the animal. Most of these animals that use the chambers of the burrows of the African Spurred Tortoise are later used as a source of food by the animal. This is particularly done in the lean period when the tortoise is very hungry and has no other option for food.

6. Are they a threatened species?

The African Spurred Tortoise species is an endangered species. There are many factors that have contributed to this.

Illicit hunting and loss of habitat are the main reasons behind this amazing species become endangered.

Research shows that there are many people buying hatchlings and young African Spurred Tortoises to rear them, but because of the long life span and kind of care required, they just get bored of them.

This makes it very important that you are very sure when you are planning to buy the African Spurred Tortoise. It is better to do all the hard work and know about them rather than taking an impulse decision of buying them and then later abandoning them.

7. Life span

The life span of a pet animal is also an important consideration when you are looking to rear and domesticate an animal. It is known that most African Spurred Tortoises outlive their pet parents. You need to be sure that you have a family structure that will look after the tortoise. The African Spurred Tortoise can live up to 100 years. Most African Spurred Tortoises live from 50 years to 100 years.

8. Understanding the behaviour of the Sulcata

If you are looking to domesticate a Sulcata, it is also important that you learn the basic characteristics and behaviour patterns of the animal. This will help you to take care of the animal in a better way.

rican Spurred Tortoise would love to move around. The
; very strong. To allow the African Spurred Tortoise to move
freely, you should have an outhouse arrangement for the
animal.

The African Spurred Tortoise loves to dig burrows. This is also a
necessity as they need to hide themselves from excessive dryness.

The African Spurred Tortoise stays comfortable in 60 F temperature
but they begin to salivate heavily when the temperature is above 105
F.

But, this saliva will drip all over their fore arms, which in turn will
help them to cool off the excessive heat. So, salivating is a good thing
for the African Spurred Tortoise.

The African Spurred Tortoise would want to roam a lot, even if it is
kept inside a house. This should be kept in mind while domesticating
the animal.

The African Spurred Tortoise is a very voracious eater. The tortoise
loves to climb. It should be made sure that they don't have access to
steep areas, so that they don't hurt themselves in a bid to climb over
the surface.

If a tortoise accidentally flips and lands on its back shell, he won't be
able to get back on its toes. There are many cases where the tortoise
develops hyperthermia. The tortoise can panic and vomit in such
cases. This can be very dangerous.

Reading the mannerisms

Even in some of the most well established homes, people are seldom
aware of the right way to approach desert animals. This results in
animals that are extremely stressed and uncomfortable. It affects
their productivity and in worst cases can provoke an attack from the
animal.

Reading the body language of your pet can really help you create
that special bond that you dream of. For instance, if a tortoise is
relaxed, he will stretch after standing up. If he is under any kind of
stress, the common behavior includes bellowing, butting and even

kicking. These behaviors are clear indicators that the immediate environment needs to be changed.

Hiding

This is something that tortoise kids are great at. They usually get into holes and spaces where they can hide. Then, they sit there really quietly. This is a natural instinct that helps them survive in a group. If there are any spaces on your property that could act as caves, you will most often find them hiding in these caves.

If you thought that the mother would be able to find her kids, you are seriously mistaken. Several studies over the years have found that kids are so good at hiding that even the moms can't find them. Most often, the mother would just wander away with no clue of where the kid is.

Several tortoise owners that I know have told me that they have been unable to locate kids for hours and sometimes overnight. Then they are found in the group the next day or under a pile of things in a secluded corner.

To be prepared for this devious hiding, you may want to use brightly coloured collars that will help you locate them easily.

Chewing

Undoubtedly, baby tortoises love to explore. Just like the babies of other species of animals, baby tortoises, too, love to explore with their mouths. So, they will chew on things and ruin them a little to learn more about them.

Climbing

Baby tortoises love to climb. In fact, they love to climb on their moms. This is allowed only with the mom and not with any other herd member. Essentially, a baby tortoise will climb only on members of the family.

So, if you see a little kid trying to climb you, then, you should feel really privileged. Climbing is a baby tortoise's way of having a good time. They actually consider anything that they can climb as toys.

This includes a fallen tree, logs, spools of cable, a picnic table and play forts that you can build for them.

Sneezing

This is a behaviour pattern that they will carry on into their adulthood. In tortoises, sneezing is not a sign of illness. It is actually a warning sign. If you see your tortoise sneezing, you must know that there is some danger (like a predator) lurking around. If the sneeze is not too tensed or alarmed, it could just be a part of a game.

Head Butting

Head butting among kids is quite different from head butting among adults. It is less aggressive and is usually playful. It is a good idea to help the kids practice head butting. If you gently push the head of a kid, he will push back.

However, you must remember never to push the forehead. This is important especially if the tortoises are a little big. It may lead to an aggressive reaction that could be dangerous for you. When you push the forehead of a tortoise, you are threatening his position in the herd.

Behavior of the adult tortoise

Among adult tortoises, all their behaviour patterns are directed towards maintaining their position in a herd. Yes, they can be playful at times. However, the main agenda is to show their worth in a herd.

Another significant behaviour change or pattern is when your tortoise is trying to send out signs that he is ready for mating or when she is nursing. Here are some common behaviour patterns you can observe in adult tortoises:

Fighting and dominance

The herd dynamics in tortoises is ever changing. Every tortoise has the ability to attain the position of the top male or the female if he or she can fight it out. So, you will see fighting quite commonly among adult tortoises.

Fighting is pronounced when new tortoises are introduced into a herd. If you do not find any animal in danger, there is no need to intervene as this is natural for tortoises.

If a female has kidded recently or if she is about to kid, she will try to improve her status in the herd. This is primarily an attempt to get her kids a better status. During these times, you cannot do much but let them fight it out even if it is too aggressive.

Tortoises also take sides when there is a fight. They tend to become helpers to the two tortoises who are in the main fight. The fights include several signs of aggression such as:

Pawing

When a female has just given birth to kids, she engages in pawing. This is her way of getting the kids to stand up and start moving around. If you think that she is attacking the kids, let me tell you that this is her way of showing that she cares.

However, you need to watch the pawing closely if you notice that the mother is very enthusiastic. In some cases, she may kill the kid accidentally.

This is not a sign of refusal either. When a mother refuses her new born, she will butt it or just ignore it.

Urinating

Urinating is a sign of when the males go into heat or into a rut. You will notice that they spray on their front legs and on their faeces. Males actually have a special attachment on the genitalia to do this.

He will even spray it into the mouth, curl up the lips and smell it. He does this to coat himself with his sticky urine that the females find attractive. Cologne for tortoises, I guess.

Developing an odour

You will notice that males begin to smell really bad as they grow. For some this smell is not exactly bad but is rather strong. The odour becomes worse with maturity.

Tortoises exhibit several other distinct herd and individual habits that you will need to get used to. You will become familiar with these habits as you observe your tortoises and interact with them.

9. Is it legal to keep an African Spurred Tortoise?

It is important to understand the legal formalities that govern the keeping of a wild animal, especially an endangered animal. There are different legal regulations in each area, so it is important to understand the regulations in your country and state specifically.

There is a rule that a veterinarian certificate is needed to keep Africa tortoises. This certificate should testify that the hatchling or the animal is free of any disease, ticks or parasite.

This is important so that there is no outbreak of any kind of virus because of the Africa tortoise. Not many states have laws about owning the tortoise except submitting the veterinarian certificate.

It should be noted here that most states have rules and regulations about the rules of a non-native species in a state. So, this needs to be kept in mind. For example, it is completely legal to keep the African Spurred Tortoise as a pet in California. But, the owner of the African Spurred Tortoise needs to apply for a permit.

The America Tortoise Rescue also caution the prospective buyers that the animal gets over 200 pounds in size and can live up to 100 years, so there is a lot of responsibility involved.

This permit is to own any desert tortoise and also to make sure the tortoise is native to the land and has not been imported illegally.

Chapter 2: Things you should know before you buy a Sulcata

If you wish to own a Sulcata or even if you already own one, it is important to understand the basic characteristics of the animal. You should know what you can expect from the animal and what you can't.

This will help you to tweak the way you behave with the Sulcata in the household, which in turn will help to build a strong bond between the pet animal and you.

Sulcatas are known to be very loyal animals. If they establish a trust factor with you, they will always remain loyal to you. This is a great quality to have in a domesticated animal.

Along with being loyal, they are also known to possess great intelligence. They will actually surprise you with their intelligence.

His unique ways and antics will leave you and the entire family in splits. If you have had a bad day, your pet will surely help you to release all the tension and enjoy life.

They are also very entertaining and playful. You can expect the entire household to be entertained by the unique gimmicks and pranks of the Sulcata. If you are looking for a pet that is affectionate, lovable and fun, then this animal is the ideal choice for you as they won't disappoint you.

In spite of all the qualities of the Sulcata, it is often termed as a high maintenance pet. If you are still contemplating whether you wish to buy a Sulcata or not, then it is important that you understand all about the maintenance of the pet, so that you can make the right choice for yourself.

While you might be extremely upbeat about bringing a tortoise home, it is necessary that you fully understand the pros and cons of bringing the animal home. Even if you bring a dog home, you have to make sure that you are all ready for the responsibilities ahead. The dog is an easy to keep animal; still its maintenance requires certain efforts from you.

A pet is like a family member. You have to make sure that the animal is taken care of. The animal should be loved in your household. If your family is not welcoming enough for the pet, the animal will lose its sense of being very quickly.

You will see a decline not just in its behaviour but also its health. You should be able to provide the pet with a safe and sound home. This is the basic requirement when planning to bring an animal home.

If an easily domesticated animal requires so much effort and attention on the part of the owner, then imagine how much effort a tortoise would want? This is not to scare you, but to make you understand that you have to know the right ways to domesticate a tortoise.

Most often than not people make the mistake of bringing an animal home without realizing its effect on one's life. When you raise a pet, your life and your family's life will also be equally affected. You can't escape that.

It is better to accept this fact and be prepared for it. The last thing that you want is to ditch the animal mid-way realizing that you can't keep it. You should also make sure that your family is comfortable with the pet.

A Sulcata is not a very easy animal to keep. It is not a very common pet. This makes it very difficult for people who are interested in keeping the animal. There is a certain life style that the animal is accustomed to. You should be able to give the animal a space that does not disturb its normal lifestyle.

Getting acquainted with pet life by reading more about it is the only way. You should gain experience by keeping relatively easier to keep animals. If you have no experience in this field then you will be relieved to learn that many first timers have done well.

But, you should always refrain from buying Sulcatas as an impulse reaction. Just because you developed an interest in Sulcatas does not mean that you should go and buy four or five of them. This will only lead to confusion on your end. This will also risk the life of these beautiful animals.

It is often advised to domesticate some simpler animals before you go on to keep a Sulcata. This will prepare you for the bigger decision of keeping a Sulcata. You will get better in terms of preparation and also confidence.

You need to give yourself three months for setting up the nursery and making it ready for the Sulcata. If you are planning to setup a nursery and buy a Sulcata at the same time, then you will only be making a mistake.

1. Why should you be so prepared when planning to bring a tortoise home?

A Sulcata is unlike most other pet animals. It requires effort from your side if you wish to keep the animal. It should be noted that because information about the animal as a pet is not too vast, there are many doubts in the minds of the people.

Many of you might wonder as to what is so special about bringing a Sulcata home. Why isn't it like getting any other pet? To clear this doubt and many other similar doubts, the following list has been created:

In regards to diet and housing, the Sulcata has some very specific needs. You should be able to understand the needs and then also fulfil them.

The animal is not a regular pet that is found in many homes. You will have to understand the ways to deal with different things related to the animal.

Such animals are different in their demeanour. Though the Sulcatas are known to be very friendly and affectionate, it will have certain traits that might differ from your usually domesticated animals.

If you are expecting your Sulcata to behave like your cat or your dog, then you should better get the dog and the cat. You should understand that the Sulcata, even after being domesticated, will have its own unique ways. It is important to let the animal be. You should not try to change the basic demeanour of the Sulcata in a bid to hand raise it.

Getting an animal home is a huge responsibility. You should be well prepared for it. There is no use crying later. All pet animals pose a challenge when you try to domesticate them. A Sulcata is all the more difficult to keep if you don't understand its requirements very clearly and precisely.

If the pet Sulcata gets sick, you should know what to do. It is important that you are not clueless and tensed in such a situation. Only a person who is well prepared will be able to take the responsibility of the animal's good health.

Anything that is not understood is very difficult. Once you understand the dos and don'ts of raising the Sulcata at your home, you will realize that it is not that difficult. All you need to do is understand the right ways to do the right things.

This chapter and the subsequent chapters will help you to prepare yourself for domesticating the Sulcata. You will be able to understand whether domesticating a Sulcata is something for you or not. It will also help you to go forward in the right direction while caring for your Sulcata.

2. The right number

If you are looking at getting more than one Sulcata or other animals along with the Sulcata, then the most obvious concern that you might have is whether this is easy. It is important that each animal in the household is compatible with each other; else there would be too much chaos and trouble, not just for the animals but also for you.

How difficult is it to domesticate more than one tortoise at a time? How many should I buy? What is the right number? Would the tortoises compete with each other for the basic necessities and the luxuries they are provided with? Would they be friendly with each other? These are the most obvious questions that would be running in the head of a person looking to buy more than one tortoise.

If you are looking at getting more than one tortoise, then you should understand the right decision would depend on a number of factors. It will depend on the following few factors:

- Space
- Personality of the tortoises
- Size considerations
- Gender considerations

Space

When looking to domesticate more than one tortoise, then one of the most important criteria that need to be kept in mind is the space that you would provide the tortoises. These animals are known to be very active. You should be able to provide them a space where they can move around without any constraints.

The important point that needs to be understood here is that domestication of even a single Sulcata will require ample space. The Sulcata will grow at a very fast pace. They need space to roam around and also to hide.

You should also understand that as the Sulcata and other tortoises grow, they need more space. If you plan on keeping more than one Sulcata, or if you want to keep other tortoises along with the Sulcata, then you would have to give them more space when they grow.

It is important that the nursery is big enough to house all the animals. The animals shouldn't have to compete amongst themselves for space. If they have to do so, it will affect their overall growth in a very negative way.

The lesser the space for the tortoises, the more difficult it will get for you to raise your pets. So, space is one factor that will always be important when you are hand raising your Sulcata or Sulcatas.

If there is one factor that drastically affects the number of tortoises that can be kept together, then it is the space that you have.

- Sulcata and other tortoises are very active in nature. They will always be on the move, so it is important to give them a good amount of space.

- If the space, which is the nursery or the outdoor house, you would provide the pets is very limited, then you need to think about your decision to get more than one tortoise.

- The Sulcata and the other tortoises get tense, stressed and unhealthy if they are not given enough space to themselves.

- It has been seen in the past that when Sulcatas and other tortoises are kept in closed quarters within a small nursery, they tend to become unhealthy and unfit. In such cases, they don't serve as ideal animals for domestication.

3. Are you prepared to domesticate a Sulcata?

You can't domesticate an animal only because the animal looks good. If this is the only reason that motivates you to bring animal such as a Sulcata home, then it is time that you rethink about your idea to domesticate the animal.

Sulcatas are not very easy to keep. They require your patience, understanding, determination, time and money. If you don't have these things to offer to your pet Sulcata, then you will not be able to raise the pet well.

If you are contemplating on the idea to bring the pet home, then it is important that you know whether you are ready or not.

- Do you have the time to take care of the pet? Do you have the patience that is required to domesticate this tortoise?

- Do you meet all the legal requirements for domesticating the pet? Is it even legal to domesticate them in your area? You might also need a permit to take it from one state to another. You should make sure that you understand all the legal formalities before you buy a pet. Different animals have different legal regulations. It is important to understand these regulations before you bring a pet animal home.

- Are you prepared for the long term commitment of raising the animal? Do you have the means and the money for it? Raising a pet animal at home is always a long term commitment. It will require your patience and hard work along with financial commitment.

- Sulcatas are known to be very intelligent and fast. You will have to be prepared for various surprises that the Sulcata will have for you. Do you have that kind of energy for them?

- These animals will hide a lot in their hiding places. You need to be prepared for this.

- These animals can be very unpredictable. They can be very moody. Do you have the patience to deal with such behaviour?

- A small area is not enough for the overall development of the Sulcata. The Sulcata needs enough space to move around in the nursery. Can you provide that kind of space in your home?

- Sulcatas can be very mischievous. They are known to make of mischief, sometimes in the night time also. If you wish to bring them home, you should be prepared for this.

- There are certain specific requirements that come along with each pet. For example, your Sulcata needs enough space in the nursery to roam around and also hide. They need to let them be if you want them to be happy.

- They have to roam around and exercise themselves. This makes it important for an adult to be around the pet almost at all times. Can you make sure that such adult supervision can be provided at your home?

- Do you have a kid under the age of 5 years at your home? Or are you planning to have a baby soon? If yes, then it might not be a good idea to buy the pet. This is because kids under the age of 5 years should not be allowed to be near the pet because of their unpredictable behaviour.

- Also, with a baby at home, you might not be able to give your pet the attention that it requires.

- If you are fond of pets that love to cuddle, then you should know that Sulcatas are not meant for this. You can't hug and cuddle an animal that lives in the desert.

- If you take them in your arms to cuddle them, they will just play and enjoy themselves.

To ensure that your Sulcata lives a happy and healthy life at your home, it is more than important that you prepare yourself in the best possible way.

You should make sure that you evaluate your resources well. It is also important to understand if your family is ready to domesticate the Sulcata or not. It might look like an overwhelming task, but it is important because bringing a new life home is a matter of great responsibility.

4. Habitat requirements of the Sulcata

It is very important that you understand the habitat requirements of the Sulcata. If you can't provide your pet a habitat that keeps him happy and safe, then you will fail as the parent of the pet. You need to make sure that the pet gets what would make it happy.

Every animal is so used to its own natural surroundings that as the owner of a new tortoise, you should make sure that you fulfil the habitat requirements of your pet animal. But before you can do so for your pet Sulcata, you should be able to understand what your Sulcata needs.

In the first few weeks, you need to be more careful as everything will be new for the pet. He will take time to get used to the new environment.

It is necessary that the infant spends as much time as possible with you. You should treat the Sulcata as your own infant baby. This is the time when you will form a bond with your pet.

But as your pet grows and matures, it needs some extra physical space for itself. It will need the space to grow and move around. In their natural habitat, Sulcatas are used to a lot of space. So, you should be able to give them the desired space even in your home. As the Sulcata grows, it would like to have a good amount of space for himself.

Designing the right nursery is very essential when domesticating a Sulcata. It is important that the enclosure is built by keeping the following points in mind:

The enclosure space should be enough for the animal. You should take into consideration that the Sulcata will grow and mature with time and accordingly his needs will change.

As the Sulcata grows, it will require more and more space. The space that you provide him should not restrict him in any way.

It should be kept as real and natural as possible. You can't keep a bird cage in a setting that is meant to be for a dog. There are specific needs for each animal, even for their habitats. It is important that you understand the habitat requirements of the Sulcata.

The Sulcata should feel comfortable and easy in the enclosure. The structure and furnishing should resemble his natural habitat. This will make the animal feel as if it is in its natural home in the wild.

The enclosure should be built in a way that is predator proof. The enclosure should be able to provide the necessary protection and safety.

You should make an in-depth analysis of the various predators that could attack the pet animal in his enclosure. You should plan the safety measures keeping in mind the strength of the predators.

The enclosure also needs to be escape proof. What if your pet decides to just escape from a gap in the enclosure? Make sure the enclosure is designed and built keeping in mind this particular point.

The enclosure should make the Sulcata emotionally safe. He needs to feel safe and secure in the setting. He needs to be comfortable and happy.

These pets are easily prone to stress. So, you should make sure that the enclosure should give him the space to de-stress and relax.

The nursery you build will depends on the space that you can afford to have. If you have no space constraints then you should make a bigger nursery for the animal. It is known that the bigger the habitat is, the better it is for the animal. These animals are very active and thus more space is always a blessing for them.

5. Precautions to be taken

You should understand that there are certain precautions that each owner should follow when domesticating a Sulcata. It is very important that you get acquainted with the dos and don'ts of keeping the animal.

You have to allow yourself the time to understand the behaviour, mannerism, habits and moods of the pet. This will allow you to avoid unpleasant incidents for your pet Sulcata.

This will help you and your family to be safe. And, this will also allow the pet Sulcata to be secure at all times.

Precautions at Home

There are many precautions that you would be required to observe at your home. These precautions will make sure that the tortoise is safe and secure. These precautions will also help you and your family to avoid any danger or injury. It is important everybody in the family is safe and sound.

Nobody should hurt the Sulcata, and nobody should be injured by him. By nature, the Sulcata is very unpredictable. If taken care of in an appropriate manner, the animal can be very friendly, but still the basic nature of the animal can't be changed.

There are a few precautions that you should follow when looking after the pet at home. These precautions will depend on the conditions of your household, whether you have children or not and whether you have other pets or not. The various scenarios and how you should take care of your pet Sulcata have been discussed in this section.

Precautions with children

If you have children at home, then you need to train your children before expecting the pet to behave in a certain way and manner. The children need to be taught about the unpredictable nature of the pet.

The children should understand that the pet is different from usual pets.

The children should understand the basic nature of the Sulcata. It is also important that they are taught what to expect and what not to. The children can't have unreal expectations that the Sulcata will start running around the house with them.

The children should be taught how to behave responsibly around the nursery. They should not put hazardous things in the nursery. Teaching the kids such things is also a great learning experience for the children. They should never to be allowed to do something nasty.

Kids can sometimes be very mischievous when in a playful mood. The child might just be trying to be a little friendly or naughty, but the animal can get irritated. While many pet animals might not react to such an action, the Sulcata can get angry and might even try to harm the kid.

You should keep children below the age of five away from the pet. The simple reason for this is that smaller kids will not understand how to behave with the pet. The kids of this age will not know the limits that they shouldn't cross with the pet. This will mean that both the kids and pet will become a danger for each other.

The kids below the age of five will not be able to understand the specific requirements and also reactions of the pet. Even if they are under adult supervision, there are high chances of a mishap. So, in the best interest of the pet and also the child, you should keep smaller kids away from the nursery containing the Sulcata.

You should make sure that the older children are around the pet only under your supervision or some adult supervision. If you kid is older, you can allow him to be around the nursery with the pet. But, you should make sure that the child understands the actions and reactions of the pet well.

You should have a discussion with the kid as to how the Sulcata is different from the rest of the pets. It is important that the kid knows the pet well. You should also make sure that you don't scare your child away. You need to inform him for his own safety.

But, that does not mean that he should be scared of his pet. When the kid understands how he should behave with the pet animal, he makes it easier for himself to have a great bond with the animal.

Precautions with other pets of the house

Since the Sulcata is in a nursery, he doesn't have much to do with other pets. A Sulcata might not be too good with other animals, such as dogs. There have been instances where the Sulcata has had problems with the dog and the cat of the house.

If the animal does not sense any potential danger from the other animal, he will be cordial with it. The Sulcata might not be very cordial with animals that are smaller in size than him.

By nature, a Sulcata sees an animal smaller than his size as a food item for him. He will have his tendency to harm this smaller pet and make it its prey. If you have very small fish, you should keep them away from the Sulcata.

The Sulcata can have his own preferences. For example, the pet Sulcata might like a certain kind of fish more than the other. The fish will also not feel very comfortable around the pet because of its high energy levels. But, the pet might not be very fond of some kinds of animals.

In particular, a Sulcata will be fond of pets that it grew up with. The Sulcata will also be fine with pets larger in size than him. If you want to have more pets in the household, make sure that they are brought around the same time and are in the similar age range. This will help them to bond well.

When you first introduce your pets to each other, you need to be extra cautious. In the beginning, keep the pets away from each other, but in the same vicinity so that they can identify with each other's smell.

If you have pets that are smaller in size as compared to your Sulcata, then you should keep the pets away from the Sulcata. For example, if you have a small turtle, rabbit, bird or a rodent in the house, they need to be away from the Sulcata for their own safety. Your Sulcata might attack the smaller pet and might try to eat it, if you are not careful enough to keep them away.

It is important to note that even if the pets in the household seem friendly and cordial to each other, you should make sure that there is some supervision when they are together. You never know when they get hostile towards each other for some petty issue.

6. Advantages and disadvantages of domesticating Sulcatas

If you are in two minds about whether you need a Sulcata or not, then this section will make it simpler for you. You should objectively look at the various advantages and disadvantages of owning a Sulcata. This will help you to make your decision.

It is important that you understand that owning any pet will have its advantages and disadvantages. You should see whether with all its pros and cons, the animal fits well into your household.

A few advantages and disadvantages of domestication of Sulcatas have been discussed in this section. If you are a prospective buyer, then this section will help you to make a wise decision.

There are people who are impressed by the adorable looks of the Sulcata. They think that this reason is enough to domesticate the animal. They believe that just because of the way the pet looks, it wouldn't require any maintenance. But, this is not true.

Domestication of a Sulcata has its unique challenges and issues. If you are not ready for these challenges, then you are not ready to domesticate the animal. Once you understand the areas that would require extra work from your side, you will automatically give your very best in those areas.

If you have already bought a Sulcata, even then this section will help you. The list of pros and cons of Sulcatas will help you to prepare yourself for the challenges that lie ahead of you. This list will help you to be a better parent to the pet and to form an ever-lasting bond with your beloved pet.

Advantages of domesticating a Sulcata:

If you are still not sure about buying a Sulcata or not, then you should know that there are many pros of domesticating this animal. They are loved by their owners and their families because of some amazing qualities that they possess.

This animal can definitely prove to be a great pet for your household and your family.

The various advantages of domesticating a Sulcata are as follows:

- The Sulcata is considered to be a very intelligent pet. It is always great to have an intelligent pet. You will be surprised many a times by his intelligent behaviour.

- A Sulcata is easy to keep if all their conditions and requirements are met. It might take you some time to understand the temperament of the animal. And, once you are able to do so, it only gets easier from there.

- Their looks make them different and adorable to look at. They are loved by one and all. Who wouldn't want to have a pet that is beautiful to look at?

- If you care well for the pet, he will also respond in a very positive way. When the Sulcata is in a happy mood, he will be stress free and relaxed. His unique ways and antics will leave you in splits.

- The Sulcata is very entertaining. If you just sit around the nursery, you are bound to have a great time.

- If there are kids in your home, then they will fall in love with this pet. But, you should monitor the interaction of the kids with the pet. This is important to keep everyone safe and sound.

- The food that the Sulcata thrives on is easily available. The Sulcata needs food only once a day. This can be great news for people who worry about feeding a variety of food to their pets three times a day.

- The Sulcatas are generally considered to be the most intelligent tortoise animals and have the most complex brain, with the capacity for both long and short term memory.

- Many people pet them when they play with them. This is generally done on the back of the Sulcata. They display a playful behaviour at such times.

- You can make a strong emotional bond with your pet and can enjoy the fruits of the bond for years to come.

- A very important point to note here is that their demeanour will depend a lot on how they are raised. The preparation has to begin right from the start. You can't expect them to suddenly become friendly after years of wrong treatment. If they are raised to be social, they will be very social.

- The Sulcatas don't overeat, so you don't have to worry in this aspect. The Sulcata will eat as much is required. They are used to eating small meals.

- One of your main concerns could be the diet of the pet. Even if you love your pet dearly, you would want to avoid any hassles while feeding the pet. You might not have the time to prepare special food all the time. In case you domesticate a Sulcata, then you will not have to worry too much about the diet. The Sulcata can be served meat with some store bought Sulcata food. There are easily available food items to ensure that the right nutrition is given to your pet.

- This pet will be the centre of attention for all the family members and also for each and every visitor of the house.

- A Sulcata has many cognitive, affective and behavioural abilities that make it similar to even the higher vertebrates. For example, you shouldn't be surprised if you notice a Sulcata holding a wine bottle and then eventually removing its cork. There are many Sulcatas that open boxes and jars easily.

- It is known that Sulcatas are very intelligent. In fact, it is said that they are most intelligent amongst all the tortoises, such as insects and worms. A Sulcata has many qualities that were earlier believed to be a domain of the vertebrates.

- They are also very entertaining and playful. You can expect the entire household to be entertained by the unique gimmicks and pranks of the Sulcata. If you are looking for a pet that is affectionate, lovable and fun, then this animal is the ideal choice for you as they won't disappoint you.

- Everybody in the house will love the pet. This is because of its very unique nature.

Disadvantages of domesticating a Sulcata:

While you have studied the advantages of domesticating a Sulcata, it is also important to learn about the various disadvantages that come along with it. Everything that has merits will also have some demerits, and you should be prepared for this.

The adorable and friendly animal has his own set of challenges when it comes to domesticating them. It is important to understand these disadvantages so that you can be better prepared for them. Following are the disadvantages of raising a Sulcata:

- The Sulcatas are very energetic by nature. This behaviour could be difficult for a first time owner.

- These animals have a very unique temperament, and it would require patience from your side to understand this kind of temperament.

- Sulcatas are capable of escaping. They are talented enough to do so. They can easily squeeze through a small gap. This gap needs to be a little larger than the shell.

- The Sulcata can be very moody. You will observe that the same animal has the capacity to sometimes be extremely playful at times and laidback at other times. This animal can be very aggressive and also laidback.

- You might have to take the decision to euthanize your pet Sulcata. You might have to take a more elaborate procedure for older and bigger Sulcatas. Bad health is generally one of the main reasons to conduct the procedure. Old age is also a very common reason to euthanize an animal. Once the Sulcata is old and incapable, it can get very difficult for him.

- The pet will depend on you for most of its needs. You should be able to identify the symptoms of various diseases in your pet to treat it well.

- If you are not careful or are inexperienced, they can lose their lives very easily.

- Kids can sometimes be very mischievous when in a playful mood. The child might just trying to be a little friendly or naughty, but the animal can get irritated. While many pet animals might not react to such an action, the Sulcata can get angry and might even try to harm the kid.

- In a bad mood, the Sulcata can even bite you or someone from your family.

- The Sulcata will spend most of its time hiding in the hiding structures that you provide him. If you have kids in your household, they might get bored with this pet very soon.

- A Sulcata is an unusual pet. It will not give you the pleasure of hugging it and playing with it. If you are looking for a pet with whom you can share physical closeness, then the Sulcata is not for you.

- Also, with a baby at home, you might not be able to give your pet the attention that it requires.

- These animals rest a lot. Though this can be an advantage for you, if you want a pet that will play with you all day, then you are in for a loss.

- The animal can gain weight very easily. They are huge and bulky.

- A lot of care has to be taken to ensure that they maintain good health. They catch disease causing bacteria and viruses very easily. Once infected, it is difficult to treat them.

- The animal can seek a lot of attention. Though the pet is solitary in its nature, there can be phases when he will require you to pamper him a lot.

- The pet can get stressed and depressed very easily. The pet is a defensive pet. He will get scared and stressed, but will not attack. This can affect him a lot.

- If spending too much money is an issue with you, then you will have to think twice before purchasing the animal.

- You should also understand the various other costs that you will encounter while raising your pet. You might have to spend a lot of money on their health.

7. Estimate of cost for domesticating a Sulcata

Domesticating an animal is not child's play. While you have to be available emotionally and physically, you also need to provide financial support.

As a prospective owner, you might be wondering about the costs that you need to prepare for when buying and then bringing up a Sulcata. You will have many doubts in your head.

As the owner and parent of the pet, you will have to make attempts to fulfil all the needs of the animal. You should also be prepared on the financial front to take care of these needs.

It is better that you plan these things well in advance. This planning will help you to avoid any kind of disappointment that you might face when there are some payments that need to be made.

To clear the various doubts in your head, you should understand the nature of the pet and also the various costs that you will incur while raising the pet.

Your pet Sulcata will have various things that will make him different from other pets. There will be specific requirements of the pet. For example, in regards to diet and housing, the animal has some very specific needs.

You should be able to understand the needs and then also fulfil them. This section will help you in understanding what you can expect in terms of finances when you are planning to bring a Sulcata to your household.

To begin with, you need money to buy the Sulcata. Once you have spent money on buying the animal, you should be ready to spend money on his domestication. You can expect to spend money on the shelter, healthcare and food of the animal.

While there are certain purchases that are only one time and fixed, you will also have to be prepared for unexpected purchases that you will have to face once in a while. You have to be ready to bear various other regular things continuously over the years.

Being well prepared is the best way to go about things. There are basically two kinds of costs that you will be looking to incur, which are as follows:

The one-time or initial costs: The initial costs are the ones that you will have to bear in the very beginning of the process of domestication of the animal. This will include the one-time payment that you will give to buy the animal.

The regular or monthly costs: Even when you are done with the one-time payments, there are some other things that you won't be able to avoid. But, these finances can be planned well in advance. You can maintain a journal to keep track of them.

The monthly costs are the ones that you will have to spend each month or once in few months to raise the Sulcata. This category includes the costs of the food requirements and health requirements of the pet.

The various regular veterinarian visits, the sudden veterinarian visits and replacement of things come under the monthly category.

The various purchases you can expect

While you are all excited to domesticate the Sulcata, you should also start planning for all that you can expect in the future while raising the pet animal. You can expect to incur the following:

Cost of buying the Sulcata

The initial cost of purchasing the Sulcata could be higher when compared with the initial cost incurred in purchasing other regular animals. If money is an issue with you, then you will have to think twice before purchasing this animal.

On the other hand, if spending money is not an issue then you should understand the other important factors for raising a Sulcata and accordingly make a decision.

You can expect to spend $100/£77.87 on a hatchling. A juvenile female will cost you $200/£155.87 to $300/£233.97. A juvenile male will cost you around $400/£316.87. The price will depend on the age and the health of the animal.

You should make sure that you get the Sulcata examined medically before buying it. The examination and tests will also add on to the initial price.

Cost of shelter

When you bring a pet home, you have to make the necessary arrangements to give it a comfortable home. The shelter of the animal will be his home, so it is important that you construct the shelter according to the animal's needs.

The Sulcata will require a good quality nursery. If their shelter is not comfortable, the pet will be restless all the time. Even if you construct a very basic nursery for the animal, it should have the necessary comfort.

This is a one-time cost, so you should not try to save money at the cost of the pet's comfort. The cost of shelter will depend on the type of the shelter. You can expect to spend anywhere between $200/£168.73 to $1000/£843.97 for the nursery of the Sulcata. A seventy gallon glass nursery can be bought at $300/£253.10.

The nursery should be ventilated well. It should also be accessorized well by you. The cage will require some basic stuff, such as live rocks, tunnels and toys.

These are the extra costs that you will have to incur in addition to the cost of the cage. This should cost you around $200/£168.73.

Heat and light source

It is important to maintain the right temperature and light cycle in a Sulcata's nursery. If this is not done, the pet can get stressed.

You should just make sure that consistent warm temperature is maintained in the nursery. The pet can get sick and unwell if you fail to maintain the right temperature and light cycle.

Depending on the type and brand of the heat and light sources, you can expect to spend $30/£22.20 to $60/£44.39.

Accessories and hiding place

As an important accessory for the pet's cage, you will have to invest in good quality tunnels. You also need to buy a hiding place for the Sulcata.

Cheap plastic materials that can have an adverse effect on the health of the Sulcata must be avoided. Similarly, toys that can be shredded or broken should also be avoided.

You also need to provide an igloo like structure for your pet to hide in. This will make him feel secure. You can prepare one at home with an old plastic tub.

Depending on your choice of toys and hiding place, you can expect to spend about $50/£36.99 to $250/£184.97.

Food

The most important factor that will affect your monthly costs is the food of the pet Sulcata. The type of the food and the quality of the food that you give to your pet will make an impact on your monthly expenditure on the pet.

A domesticated Sulcata will mostly be fed good quality grass. You might also have to include various supplements to give your pet overall nourishment.

This is important because if the animal does not get all the appropriate nutrients in the right amount, his health will suffer, which again will be an extra cost for you. So, make sure that you provide all the necessary nutrients to your pet animal.

The kinds of food that you feed your pet will also affect the exact food cost that you encounter per month. You should remember that the more lax you are regarding the money that goes into food costs, the more the amount of money that would go into health care.

If your pet is well fed, it will not fall sick that often. This will automatically reduce the amount of money that you would have to spend on the veterinarian and medication.

You will have some options when it comes to feeding your Sulcata. You can choose amongst those options, depending on the availability of the items in your region and also the price of the food items.

You can expect to spend about $75/£63.28 to $300/£253.10 every month on the food of the Sulcata.

Cost of health care

It is important to invest in the health of a pet animal. This is necessary because an unhealthy animal is the breeding ground of many other diseases in the home. Your pet might pass on the diseases to other pets if not treated on time. This means danger for the pets and also the members of the family.

You will have to take the Sulcata to the veterinarian for regular visits on his health. He will be able to guide you regarding any medications that the pet may need.

It is advised that for the very first year of domestication, you are extra careful regarding the health of the animal.

You should also be prepared for unexpected costs, such as sudden illness or accidents in the Sulcata. Health care is provided at different costs in different areas. So, the veterinarian in your area could be costlier than the veterinarian in the nearby town.

You should work out all these costs right in the beginning, so that you don't suffer any problems later. Realizing that you can't keep the animal and giving it up is never a good idea.

You should understand that taking care of these animals will require special skills. You should make sure that the veterinarian that you consult for your pet Sulcata is experienced in handling desert animals.

You should also be prepared to spend more money on their health than what you would have spent on other pet animals. It is believed that you should have an extra $1000/£843.97 saved for your Sulcata's emergencies. He might require an operation or surgery because of a disease.

Other costs

Although the main costs that you will encounter while raising your pet have already been discussed, but there will be some extra costs that you will have to take care of. Most of these costs are one-time costs.

You will have to spend money to buy stuff such as rocks for the pet. You can expect to spend $100/£73.99 to $250/£184.97 on these costs. The cost will depend on the wear and tear and the quality of the products.

In order to keep track of the costs that could be awaiting you, you should regularly check the various items in the nursery of the pet. If you think that something needs to be repaired or replaced, you should go ahead and do it.

Chapter 3: Myths about the African Spurred Tortoise

While you might be extremely upbeat about bringing a tortoise home, it is necessary that you fully understand the pros and cons of bringing the animal home. Even if you bring a dog home, you have to make sure that you are all ready for the responsibilities ahead. The dog is an easy to keep animal; still its maintenance requires certain effort from you.

A pet is like a family member. You have to make sure that the animal is taken care of. The animal should be loved in your household. If your family is not welcoming enough for the pet, the animal will lose its sense of being very quickly.

Though the African Spurred Tortoises are gaining popularity around the world, there is still a lot of confusion regarding this animal. This leads to many myths that spread the wrong information. This chapter will help you bust some myths around the African Spurred Tortoise, and you will also learn some important facts about the animal.

Myth 1- The African Spurred Tortoise and the spur thigh tortoises are the same.

It should be noted here that African Spurred Tortoise is often confused with another popular tortoise called the spur thighed tortoise. But, this is nothing but a myth.

These two types of tortoises have front legs with enlarged scales and also similar names, leading to the confusion.

To avoid his confusion, the African Spurred Tortoise is also referred to as the sulk tortoise owing to its scientific name of Geochelone Sulcata.

Myth 2- The African Spurred Tortoises are found in all desert regions.

There are many people that believe that the African Spurred Tortoises are easily available all around the world in various desert regions. But, this is not the truth.

As a prospective owner, it is important that you understand that habitat of your pet animal. This will help you to give better care to the animal.

It is known that the African Spurred Tortoises are only found in northern Africa that too at the south edge of the Sahara desert.

Myth 3- The tortoise is not a grumpy animal.

There are many people that believe that the African Spurred Tortoise will be very docile and good tempered at all times. Though the tortoise is a great pet, the pet can have some mood fluctuations.

The male African Spurred Tortoise is particularly known to have a grumpy attitude. The male can be authoritative and would try to pick fights with other male African Spurred Tortoises.

The male, when in an argumentative and aggressive mood, can be seen ramming his fellow male African Spurred Tortoises. He will make all kind of noises and will grunt loudly. He can also be seen whistling.

It should also be noted that the males are grumpy just by nature. In fact, the young ones can be seen competing with each other to flip one another.

Myth 4- The African Spurred Tortoise can't go without drinking or eating even for a day.

The African Spurred Tortoise can't go without drinking or eating even for a day is nothing but a myth. There is no truth in this.

Many research papers over the years have shown that an African Spurred Tortoise is capable of going without consuming food or even water for many weeks. These animals are able to sustain well in such conditions.

In the wild, the Sulcata has to survive harsh weather more often than not. The body of the animal is adapted according to its environment.

The African Spurred Tortoise might have to stay for longer duration in burrows and other warm areas where food is not readily available. The animal can sustain well in such conditions.

It is also interesting to know that at any given time an African Spurred Tortoise can drink a lot of water, almost fifteen percent of its body weight. One can imagine how much water an African Spurred Tortoise is capable of consuming.

Myth 5- An African Spurred Tortoise can't dig owing to its size

There is another myth that is widely circulated that states that the sheer size of the Sulcata makes incapable of digging burrows. The truth is just the opposite.

The African Spurred Tortoises dig burrows. They do this mainly in the monsoon season from July to November. It is basically preparation to face the dry spell in the summers.

These burrows are useful throughout the year. The mid-day temperatures in the Sahel region are very high. The tortoises use the burrows to save themselves from these high temperatures.

An African Spurred Tortoise is very skilled in making burrows. A typical burrow constructed by the Sulcata can have a vertical depth of 20 feet and horizontal length of over 30 feet.

The burrow is very deep so that the tortoise can feel safe and also because the temperature will be relatively stable. The temperature outside can fluctuate a lot throughout the day. The depth of the burrows also allows for humidity levels over fifty percent.

As stated earlier, an African Spurred Tortoise is very skilled in making burrows. The burrows are so skilfully divided into tunnels and chambers.

The different chambers are well connected by different tunnels. This gives the burrow a definite structure.

Myth 6- The African Spurred Tortoise is so big that the animal has no danger of predation

The African Spurred Tortoises are gaining popularity as a pet around the world, but there is still a lot of confusion regarding this animal.

This leads to much confusion in the mind of people that spread the wrong information.

The African Spurred Tortoise is a large animal, but that does not mean that it is not threatened by other animals. There are a few predators that are known to hunt these tortoises in the wild.

You will be surprised to know that large and ferocious dogs and even cats are capable of killing these African Spurred Tortoises.

It is also known that some nomadic groups in Sahel also look in the deserts to hunt them down. They do this to trade the body parts of the animal. The body parts are in high demand in Japan to be used in many important medicines.

Myth 7- The African Spurred Tortoise can get dehydrated easily because of the hot and dry temperatures it is exposed to.

It is a myth that the African Spurred Tortoise can get dehydrated easily because of the hot and dry temperatures it is exposed to.

Many pet parents believe that the African Spurred Tortoise can get dehydrated by such temperatures. But, this is not true. The animal is used to excessive dryness and heat. This will not impact him in a negative way.

The African Spurred Tortoise can obtain most of its water requirements with the help of the food that it consumes. But, you should also keep a bowl of water in case the African Spurred Tortoise wants to drink.

The African Spurred Tortoise hails from the hot equatorial Africa. You can imagine the kind of environment the animal must be exposed to. It is important to provide the animal with an environment which closely resembles its natural habitat.

The African Spurred Tortoise should be allowed to have access to basking temperatures. The surface temperatures should be around 100 degrees.

Chapter 4: Reproduction in Sulcatas

As a new owner of a tortoise, you might be interested in the reproduction cycle and procedure of the Sulcata. The reproduction in Sulcatas is known to be very challenging. But, it will get easier to understand once you equip yourself with all the right knowledge. This chapter is meant to clear all your doubts regarding the reproduction in Sulcatas.

You should know that breeding in Sulcatas is defined as the production of an offspring by mating by the Sulcatas. It is important to understand the breeding patterns of your pet animals. How well you understand the mating patterns of your pet will also determine how well you look after the pet.

Keeping and caring for an animal in your home also means that you understand each aspect of their lives. Reproduction is an important aspect of any animal's life. This is the way the species can continue to survive.

You can't and shouldn't ignore such an important aspect of the Sulcata's life. You should also understand the effect of reproduction on the life of the Sulcata. This will allow you to understand the life of the tortoise in greater depth.

When you are conducting controlled mating at your home, there are many things that you will have to take care of. You should make sure that the male and the female Sulcata are ready for mating. They should have reached the right maturity level.

After they have mated, you should be ready to take care of the female and the eggs. It is also important that you take care of the nesting requirements of the Sulcatas once the mating is over and the female pet Sulcata is pregnant.

1. Basic information regarding breeding

When you get a Sulcata home, it is very important to understand its breeding cycle. Each animal species has their unique breeding habits and patterns. When you are looking to take care of your pet well, you should also lay enough emphasis on understanding his breeding patterns.

For certain species of the tortoises, there are many rituals attached to mating. On the other hand, there are a few species that go about mating in a very subdued manner. There is nothing exciting about the entire process.

A Sulcata will have the inner urge or desire to indulge in mating once it grows up. This is natural in all species. It is important to understand the effect of reproduction or mating on Sulcatas.

Both the male and female Sulcata die after mating, but the duration of their lives after mating differs. It is known that a male Sulcata will not be able to survive for more than a few months after it has mated with a female Sulcata.

A female Sulcata also can't make it too far after it has mated with the male Sulcata. It is said that a female Sulcata will die after the eggs that it laid have hatched.

You should understand the natural mating behavior of your pet animals. This will help you to do the right thing when breeding them. This chapter is meant to equip you with all the knowledge that you might need for mating your Sulcatas.

A good breeder will always encourage you to thoroughly understand the sexual tendencies of your Sulcatas so as to not commit any mistake in the future. You need to know how often and in what conditions your Sulcatas can reproduce.

In the wild, the baby Sulcatas have higher chances of survival in a warm environment. This means that the Sulcatas enter their mating cycle in the right temperatures. You can expect the same when the Sulcatas are domesticated.

When a Sulcata is in its natural environment, the extra amount of light during the summers and also spring brings about a change in its body. The male and female Sulcata get sexually active during this time.

A male Sulcata will display changes in his behavior. He will seem more aggressive and restless. This is due to the sex hormones that have become active in his body. This is how you can identify if your male pet animal is ready to mate or not.

If you are keeping a Sulcata, you should also make an effort to learn about the breeding patterns of these animals. This will enhance your understanding of the animal.

There are many animals that have a specific breeding season. These animals complete the mating process and other subsequent processes during this season. But, in case of the Sulcata tortoise, there is no specific breeding season.

The tortoise can mate all through the year. But, there are certain factors that affect the mating process.

2. Factors affecting the mating process

Rainy season brings about a change in the inactive African Spurred Tortoises. The tortoises begin to forage and also replace the lost reserves so that they are ready for reproduction.

It is this season when the tortoises breed and lay their eggs. The Sulcatas don't have a season exclusively for breeding.

It is observed that during the beginning of the autumn season, the morning temperatures are quite cool. These temperatures are ideal for the Sulcatas that are ready to breed.

The population of the male African Spurred Tortoises is smaller. The breeding can occur throughout the year if the male African Spurred Tortoise has an encounter with the female African Spurred Tortoise, but that does not happen often.

During the dry spell, the tortoises are really inactive so chance encounters don't happen. At the beginning and also toward the rainy season in the region, the Sulcatas are very active so there is a probability of a male encountering a female Sulcata.

3. Mating process

It is observed that during the beginning of the autumn season, the morning temperatures are quite cool. These temperatures are ideal for the Sulcatas that are ready to breed.

If you are wondering what the process is that leads to mating, you will be quite surprised. A male Sulcata will court a female by actually ramming them.

The male tortoise will push the female towards obstacles. He would try to get in front of the female by ramming her.

If you are confused by such a hostile behaviour of the male Sulcata, then you would be surprised to know that the intention of the male is to stop the female for a significant period of time so that mating can occur.

If the female Sulcata stays for long enough, the male will mount on her. This is the beginning of the mating process. The entire process is carried forward with many loud and hoarse grunts.

The breeding process can be expected between November to May. The nesting process by the female tortoise is done generally at the base of the bushes. The female can lay up to 24 eggs. It is known that the eggs that are deposited are usually less than 24.

The size of the eggs that the female tortoise lays and the number of tortoise eggs that are deposited have a correlation. A large clutch size will lead to smaller eggs. On the other hand, a small clutch size will result in larger sized eggs.

These eggs will lead to hatchlings. It is known that it usually takes 100 to over 200 days for the hatchlings to appear. The exact time will depend on the time when the eggs were deposited.

There are many factors that will affect the growth of the hatchlings. All these and more will be discussed in the subsequent chapters.

It is important to learn here that the young Sulcatas are quite large. They don't spend time in the nest and will be very eager to leave it. The young ones will show tremendous growth in the first two years.

The resources available to the hatchlings also effect the growth of the young ones. A scarcity of the resources can have a hard effect on their growth process.

It is also known that the young ones can gain weight in excess of two pounds after the very first year. These young tortoises attain about seven pounds after the second year.

4. Nesting for the African Spurred Tortoise

African Spurred Tortoise has a distinct pattern even for nesting. It is important that you understand clearly this process and the subsequent ones.

After the mating is performed in a captive environment, the nesting can be expected anywhere between six to eight weeks. There are a few signals that will indicate that the African Spurred Tortoise is going in the nesting period.

The female Sulcata will dig a huge pit. This will be done with the help of the front legs of the animal. The pit would resemble the start point of a burrow because of its depth.

The female will try to dig a pit as deep as possible. It is sloped in a way that one end is deeper than the other. This is done against some object such as a wall.

After this process is over, the female African Spurred Tortoise will back into the pit. She will then excavate its egg chamber. Her rear legs help her to do so.

The female will neatly deposit the eggs in the pit. She will also cover the nest appropriately. It should be noted here that the female takes her own good time to do the entire process. Records show that it can take hours for the African Spurred Tortoise female to go through the process.

There are some species of animals that are very intense about the nest protection. Though it is observed that most tortoises are not that intense, the African Spurred Tortoise does exhibit some degree of protection towards the nest.

Each tortoise is different from the other, so you can expect to be taken by surprise by your female African Spurred Tortoise. They can be very aggressive when it comes to protection. You need to watch out for this kind of behaviour from the female Sulcata.

It is important to leave the female African Spurred Tortoise alone at this time because this is an emotionally taxing time for the female. If you, your family, other tortoises or other animals move around the pit at this time, the female will get very hostile towards you.

Various aggressive behaviours have been reported by many African Spurred Tortoise pet parents when the female was nesting.

Some females will be less aggressive and more methodical during this period. They will be very particular about the pit that they are digging.

According to a recorded incident, the female Sulcata ran almost 50 yards towards the person in a bid to bite him because he thought he was a threat. The female was seen pulling her head inside the shell before ramming things that were around her. This was a display of anger.

According to another incident, the female Sulcata kept banging her shell into the body of the pet parent. You can imagine a 100 pound tortoise getting so aggressive.

If you ever face such a situation, it is important to recede. Don't try to confront the female African Spurred Tortoise in any way. This will only lead to more aggressive behaviour from the pet animal.

The best you can do is to leave the spot that very moment, There is no way you can pacify the female tortoise except from just leaving.

It is important that you don't leave any other pet animals near the female tortoise at this time. Even the male tortoise should be kept away.

As soon as the potential danger recedes, the African Spurred Tortoise will get back to the nest by giving it a cover. Sometimes, a female exhibits such behaviour towards empty nests.

It is important to note here that a female African Spurred Tortoise is capable of producing many clutches in a single year.

There are a few female African Spurred Tortoises that produce five clutches in a single season. This is the highest recorded number from a single female.

If a female tortoise produces more than one clutch in a single season, the clutches are separated by a minimum of thirty to forty days.

If you are curious to know the size of a clutch then you need to know that a single clutch can have twelve to twenty four eggs. The number can go up to as high as forty two eggs in a clutch.

5. Incubation

It is important that the eggs are collected as soon as possible. This will help to protect the eggs from predators. There are a few things that you need to observe that will ensure that the eggs are safe.

Once the eggs are laid, they need to be collected. These eggs should be safely collected in a clean container. This will protect the eggs from potential threats.

This container needs to be buried. You should bury it carefully midway of the vermiculite. It also needs to be moistened with the help of water. The ratio needs to be maintained at 1 to 0.5. This ratio is by weight.

The incubation needs to be done at the right temperature. A failure to maintain the right temperature will lead to errors during this critical phase.

The right temperature for incubation of the eggs of the African Spurred Tortoise is 82 degrees Fahrenheit to 86 degrees Fahrenheit. The temperature needs to be kept constant throughout.

When the eggs are exposed to a continuous stream of correct temperature, the eggs will hatch properly and in due time. The eggs typically take anywhere between 100 days to 120 days to hatch completely.

The eggs in the clutch will mostly hatch together. This process can take some time. The pace of the various eggs to hatch can also vary, so you need to be patient.

The eggs will take a few days. In most cases, they take a few weeks, although in some cases it has been seen that the eggs take months to hatch. The first egg might take a few days to hatch and the last one to hatch might take a few months. This needs to be clearly understood.

You should make sure that the hatchlings are left in the incubator undisturbed. This should be done until the yolks of the eggs are absorbed.

After the yolks of the hatchlings are all absorbed, you an place them in a tray. They should be carefully placed over moistened paper towels. They should be left there until the plastrons seal effectively.

6. Female or male

If you are keen to know how the sex of the African Spurred Tortoise is determined and various factors that help in ascertaining the sex of the tortoise, then you should know that there are many studies been conducted to know the exact factors that affect the sex of the African Spurred Tortoise.

According to a widely popular belief, the temperature that the eggs are exposed to during the hatching process determines the sex of the African Spurred Tortoise. There is no definite proof of this.

In some places, the Sulcatas are sexed with a carapace that is straight and is about twelve inches in length. But, this can be very difficult.

As their bodies develop, concave plastrons develop on the male African Spurred Tortoise. The tails of the males are very thick. If you compare the male and female tail in the African Spurred Tortoise, the males have longer tails.

Female African Spurred Tortoises also have long tails when compared with other tortoise species, the tails are relatively longer in the African Spurred Tortoise females.

7. Challenges of the birthing process

The breeding of Sulcatas is often said to be challenging. The reason behind this is because these animals were earlier not domesticated and are still widely found in the wild. This makes it difficult for people to observe and then understand their breeding and mating routines.

Even after the domestication of tortoises started, there are many species of tortoises that are not domesticated. Not much is known about the domestication of such species.

You should understand the following points to understand the mating and the birthing process of the Sulcata.

It is known that the male Sulcata plays an active part in the mating process. In fact, the female counterpart does not have much of a role to play.

The females remain extremely timid and passive during the entire process of mating.

The male Sulcata is known to be focussed and concentrated towards the act from the start to the end. The female would have conceived by the end of the mating process.

It is said that after the female conceives, she goes into a phase of gestation. If the female Sulcata is observed after her gestation period, you will come to know when she will give birth to another Sulcata.

She will be seen cleaning her abdominal area. In fact, the female spends many hours in this cleaning process. She will lick her abdominal area and make a trail from there up till the stomach.

Once the contractions begin, the female Sulcata can be seen looking for a vertical object for support. In the wild, she would look for a wooden log or a tree. If someone is around during the contraction phase of the female Sulcata, it is always good to keep something that the female can use in her vicinity.

This phase will go on for a long time. The female Sulcata will experience contractions every now and then. This will be difficult for her, but this is the only way to bring the new life into form.

After this, the female will get ready to give birth to an infant, who will depend on her for a long time for all his needs.

The small and wriggling infant will be born soon. It should be noted that when the infant is born, he is still attached to the mother physically.

After giving birth to the baby Sulcata, the mother will move and come in a sitting position. This is to aid the baby Sulcata to reach the mother Sulcata.

Soon after the mother sits, the infant can be seen floating and climbing towards the pouch of his mother Sulcata. In almost ten minutes, the baby is able to get inside. After reaching the pouch, the baby Sulcata makes sure that it immediately attaches its body to the teat of his mother.

The various species have their own specific duration of attaching and remaining in the pouch. No matter which species is in consideration, the infant will come out in a few weeks. .

8. Understanding a young African Spurred Tortoise

It should be noted here that a young Sulcata is capable of growing up very fast. A Sulcata has a life span of many years. It shows rapid growth right from the very beginning.

A juvenile Sulcata can rapidly increase its body size. The food that you serve the Sulcata will be utilized properly by the body of the animal.

It is estimated that Sulcatas, even the young ones, are capable of increasing the mass of their body by over five percent every single day. In fact, after the Sulcata dies, it weighs almost one third of the weight of all the food that it had eaten in its life.

When you bring a pet home, it is more like a new member of the family. It is very important that you take time to understand the various stages in the pet's life, as each stage will demand different care and methods.

In case you decide to breed your Sulcata, you will face the situation of where you will take care of a young one. There are many people who buy young Sulcatas from the breeders who also have to face the same situation.

Hand rearing a baby animal can be very tricky, but if you pay attention to the details, it will be fun and interesting. You should take care of a few things to make sure that your baby Sulcata is taken care of.

If, for some reason, a mother is not capable of taking care of the young, then the babies can be given to another female that is in the same age group as the mother. This should be done in the first few days of kindling, preferably the first three to four days.

It should also be noted that body temperature regulation is very important for a young pet, but a baby animal is unable to regulate the temperature of his body. You will have to make sure that the baby Sulcata is experiencing the right temperatures.

He has to be warm at all times, but make sure that the temperature does not get too hot, as this can also be harmful for the Sulcata. You will have to constantly monitor the temperature so that it does not overheat the infant.

9. Raising and rearing baby Sulcata

You need to be well prepared when you hand rear an infant. It can be very challenging if you don't get your basics right. While you might have learnt it all, there are a few important points that need to be remembered taking care of the infant Sulcata.

To hand rear the infant Sulcata, you would need to follow the following points:

There is a simple formula for the feed that you should be giving your infant. You should make sure that the water you use to prepare the formula has been cooled after heating it.

It should be noted that you should not use cold water because it is not right for the formula. You should also not use boiling water because it can again destroy the mineral content of the formula.

A simple way to make use of the water is to boil the water, and then let the boiled water cool down. This information can be used to plan the further activities.

The animal can easily change color. It can harm you if you are not careful. It can easily pass through smallest of holes. These tricks make the Sulcata very smart and prepared.

It should be noted that a mature male will have an organ named the ligula. This looks like a mit on an arm. It is easy to recognize this particular organ with the eye.

It is important that you take care of your pet's health. The pet will depend on you for most of its needs. It will not be able to tell you if it is facing any discomfort regarding its health. You should be able to identify the symptoms of various diseases in your pet to treat it well.

If you take care of the diet of the pet, you can save him from many deadly diseases. You should make sure that the pet lives in a healthy environment. These simple things will help you to keep the pet healthy and fit.

You should also be able to diagnose any symptoms of injury in your pet. If you can treat him in your home, then you should do it very carefully. In case you have any doubts, you should take the pet to the doctor.

Chapter 5: Housing a Sulcata

Domesticating a Sulcata requires a lot of planning. You can't buy one from the store and domesticate it without a proper plan because that won't work for you.

It is always advised to read more and more about the subject to get yourself acquainted and fully prepared. It is also suggested to start with other simpler animals. This will give you some experience.

Keeping a tortoise is a different challenge as compared to keeping regular pet animals. There is no denying this fact. To make things smoother for you, it is a better idea to start with animals that are easier to keep.

It is always a good idea to keep other tortoises before you can keep Sulcata. This will help you gain some insight and experience.

You should also remember that there are no rights and wrongs here. Though it is advised to start with relatively easier animals, this does not mean that you can't keep Sulcata right in the beginning.

There are many people who have managed to keep Sulcatas without any prior experience of tortoise life. It completely depends on you and your choice. Just be aware of the pros and cons of both.

In any case you have to do some preparation before you can keep a Sulcata. It is suggested to keep some three months aside preparing the nursery for the Sulcata in your home.

This chapter will help you with an equipment list that will allow you to prepare the home for the new pet that you will bring to your place. Proper care is of utmost importance for the pet.

It is known that many tortoises lose their lives because of the lax attitude of their owners. If you are not careful, you will only lose your pet Sulcata.

If you don't have any experience of keeping a huge animal, then you need to understand this step very well. It is important to understand the cycle. This is a way of ensuring that your animals lead a happy life.

Improper equipment can kill an animal. If you are a novice when it comes to keeping a Sulcata then you need to pay all the more attention to this step. A small error on your part can kill the poor animal.

There are many people that want to keep a Sulcata at home. The first question that bothers these people is how they will manage to keep the right environment in the nursery and house. This will require consistent efforts from your side, but in turn you will be able to keep your Sulcata happy and healthy.

When you go to buy a Sulcata, you will be surprised to learn that many of the shops that sell these animals have no knowledge of the species they are selling. These shops will refer to the Sulcatas with general names such as tortoise.

You should never buy from these shops. It is better to know the species of the tortoise. This will affect the way you keep the Sulcata.

1. Building the right home

As you know by now, the African Spurred Tortoises are amongst the largest tortoises in the world. This simply calls for special arrangements to house them.

You need to make proper arrangements to make sure that the animal is housed well. You will have to make sure that they don't miss the natural environment of their habitat.

You should also know that the hatchlings and juvenile tortoises are very small. They will require special arrangements to keep them safe and sound.

If you are planning to buy an African Spurred Tortoise or a hatchling, you need to make sure that you understand the housing needs of the African Spurred Tortoise.

There are many people that just buy the African Spurred Tortoise as an impulse decision. This is not the right way. It can be detrimental for the wellbeing of the animal and you will also suffer because of this. You should be sure that you want this animal as a pet.

2. Indoor vs outdoor accommodation

The first question whenever you have to house a wild animal is whether you can keep the animal inside the house, or you need a special enclosure outside the house. You might also be tormented by such questions.

It is important to understand here that the young ones can be safely housed inside the house. They should be kept safe and warm inside the right enclosure.

While the younger one can be safely kept inside the house, the adult African Spurred Tortoise needs outdoors. You can't expect to keep such a big animal inside a house. Also, the animal needs to be outside to stimulate its natural environment.

This chapter will help you to understand all that needs to be done to build the right enclosure for the African Spurred Tortoise. This will help you to keep the pet African Spurred Tortoise happy and in turn, healthy.

Indoor nursery

The African Spurred Tortoise requires a constant temperature range to be maintained throughout the year.

It is important to understand here that the young ones can be safely housed inside the house. They should be kept safe and warm inside the right enclosure.

The young African Spurred Tortoise requires around four feet of space. But, the more space that you provide, the better it is. The African Spurred Tortoise requires more space as they grow.

The tortoise can grow very fast. Before you know it, the animal would have increased in weight and size. It would get troublesome for you at that time. So, it is better to provide ample space to allow the African Spurred Tortoise to grow uninhibited and in the best possible way.

You can create a small nursery at home where you can place the animal. You can buy such a nursery from any pet shop that houses tortoises. They are easily available.

You can also create a nursery at home. You can use a tortoise trough for this purpose. You can also use a nursery, reptile cage or plastic storage box.

Such a nursery can help you to house the Sulcata for the first four to five years of its life. After the five years, the tortoise will be more than twelve inches.

It will be very difficult to house such a big animal in a nursery arrangement. It will require more space.

Outdoor spaces

African Spurred Tortoises gain weight very quickly and before you know it your young African spurred will be 100 pounds in weight. Their carapaces are over 30 inches in length. So, it is better to provide ample of space to allow the African Spurred Tortoise to grow uninhibited and in the best possible way.

If you are looking at proving a housing space for an adult African Spurred Tortoise, then you should know that the animal will require over 60 square feet of space. If the space is larger, it is always better.

In fact, most pet owners of African Spurred Tortoises will advise you have 120 square feet or even 180 square feet of space for the this big and huge animal.

This is an important consideration when you are looking to domesticate an African Spurred Tortoise. If you don't have the desired outdoor space, there is no point in domesticating the African Spurred Tortoise. You will only make the animal's and your life difficult.

You should also make sure that the area where you live is suitable for the African Spurred Tortoises. The region should have a dry and warm climate. This is the only way to let the African Spurred Tortoise thrive well.

3. Building housing areas

Shelterbelts cannot be created overnight. It may take several months for the shelterbelt to grow properly. In case you do not have trees to protect your tortoise during adverse weather conditions, here are a few housing options that you can try:

- **Single slope, open sided sheds:** This is the most typical housing option. It is suitable for any animal that you have. It is easy to build and is also economical. When you build an open sided shelter, make sure that the open end faces south in the winter to block any wind. You also have the option of partitioning the pole barns to make sure that the animals are kept at a distance easily.

- **Clear span open sided shelter:** You can open any side of this shelter as per the weather. You have a gable end that should be open when there is any rain or snow. With the gable end open, you have more depth in the bay area, protecting the animal from winds. The back end of this shelter may become damp and will require ventilation and lighting.

- **An unused barn:** This structure can be built but it is a better option if you already have one on your farm. You can renovate it as per the requirement of your tortoise. This is cheaper than installing a whole new structure.

- **Hoop barn:** This is possibly the most expensive type of shelter for your pet. But it does provide a lot of protection in cold conditions. However, in the warmer months, ventilation can be a problem. If you have ample grazing space for your animals, this is not really a big concern. A hoop barn looks almost like a green house with a roof that is arched.

Make sure that the design is simple and practical to maintain it well. You must have enough space to make a feed yard to keep the animals comfortable and socialize properly.

The flooring should be covered with some substrate that can absorb waste. The best option is hay. Mud is not a good idea, especially in winter. Evaporation is lower with mud and if the draining is improper, it can become a harbor for several microbes. If the floor is already made of mud, adding bedding like hay can be a good option.

The selected area for housing should be higher than the rest of the land. That will help you get rainwater and waste out easily.

There should be ample light and air supply in the shelter. Sunlight is extremely necessary to keep the shelter dry and prevent any germs or viruses from breeding.

Try to build a shelter in an area that is surrounded by trees. This helps provide additional shade and shelter to the animals.

There should be a good drainage system inside the shelter to make sure that there is no dampness whatsoever. Trash and excreta in the shelter will lead to the growth of viruses, parasites and insects like mosquitos and flies.

The shelter should be covered with some form of fencing. We will discuss the options in the next section.

It is a good idea to create a separate area of housing to keep any injured or sick tortoises. This should be a quiet and dry area to prevent any stress.

You must keep the shelter ready before you bring your African Spurred Tortoise home. Make sure that it suits the requirements based on the number of animals and even the age and gender. Younger animals will need a shelter that is stronger as they tend to have more energy which means that they are able to apply more force on the walls.

4. Bedding options

The bedding that you place in the housing should be made from a material that will be able to keep the African Spurred Tortoises warm and dry throughout. It must also be easy to clean.

If the material that you are using has the property of retaining water, then you will notice that it will be very hard to maintain the shelter well. So, for the best results, you must use the following bedding options in your shelter:

Pine Shavings

This is the most preferred type of bedding option as African Spurred Tortoises simply love it. It is ideal for smaller herds. The best thing about pine shavings is that they are highly absorbent. They have the ability to soak in not only the wetness but also the odour of the poop.

They help you manage the litter well. Additionally, pine shavings are also very soft and light. The shavings are extremely easy to replace. They are also highly affordable and easily available. If you are buying pine shavings online, make sure you don't get confused between chips and shavings. Pine chips are terrible bedding options.

Straw and Hay

This is a popular bedding choice among people who have small farms. The reason that it is so popular is that it is extremely affordable and really durable.

It is also a good absorbent that has the ability to soak the wetness and also soak the odour. The quality of the straw and hay is important. If you compromise on this, the straw will remain moist, making the shelter smell really bad.

Shredded Paper

In case you run out of your regular bedding material, shredded paper can make a great alternative. It is also considered one of the most popular trends among owners. This is not only a good bedding option but is also a great way to recycle paper.

The best thing is that you will never run out of it. All you need to do is shred the newspaper in your home into small pieces and lay it on the floor neatly. Newspaper shredding is a great absorbent like any other bedding material. The African Spurred Tortoises will not be harmed by it at all.

Dirt

Dirt is a really interesting option for shelter bedding. The first and the most important thing is that dirt is completely natural. Hence, it will not harm the animals even a little. Sand along with the poop can make great compost.

Sawdust

This is a rather novel idea in the world of pet keeping. Sawdust is great as it is really soft. Sawdust also has a natural smell that keeps the coop fresh all day long. During the colder months, sawdust makes a great bedding option as it can be really warm.

The only disadvantage with saw dust is that it retains water. It is also prone to bacteria. So, you must make sure that you change the sawdust regularly if you choose to use it.

When you are choosing the bedding option for the shelter, there is one more thing that you must consider. If your African Spurred Tortoises are sharing the space with another pet, you must avoid bedding that will not suit the other animal.

5. Dry and warm temperature

You should also make sure that the area where you live is suitable for the African Spurred Tortoises.

You don't want to bring in an animal and then give him an environment where he can't thrive.

The region where you wish to domesticate the tortoise should have a dry and warm climate. This is the only way to let the African Spurred Tortoise thrive well.

The Sulcata hails from the hot equatorial Africa. You can imagine the kind of environment the animal must be exposed to. It is important to provide the animal with an environment which closely resembles its natural habitat.

The African Spurred Tortoise should be allowed to have access to basking temperatures. The surface temperatures should be around 100 degrees.

Sometimes, it is not possible to give the animal such a high temperature just by exposing it to the sun. In such cases, you should have basking lights in your outdoor enclosure.

The African Spurred Tortoise produces the vitamin D3 in its body with the help of sunshine. If vitamin D3 is absent in the African Spurred Tortoise's body, the calcium in the diet would not be absorbed properly.

If you are rearing an African Spurred Tortoise inside your house, the animal should be exposed to full spectrum lighting. This must include UVB part of the spectrum at the basking spot.

It is also advised to avoid misting the African Spurred Tortoise's cage. The enclosure needs to be kept dry.

Many pet parents believe that the African Spurred Tortoise can get dehydrated by such temperatures. But, this is not true. The animal is used to excessive dryness and heat. This will not impact him in a negative way.

Also, the African Spurred Tortoise can obtain most of its water requirements with the help of the food that it consumes. But, you should also keep a can of water in case the African Spurred Tortoise wants to drink.

6. Protection from predation

The African Spurred Tortoise is a large animal, but that does not mean that it is not threatened by other animals. There are a few predators that are known to hunt these tortoises in the wild.

You will be surprised to know that large and ferocious dogs and even cats are capable of killing these African Spurred Tortoises.

It is also known that some nomadic groups in Sahel also look in the deserts to hunt them down. They do this to trade the body parts of the animal. The body parts are in high demand in Japan to be used in many important medicines.

It is important that appropriate protection is given to the African Spurred Tortoise. The tortoise should be safe from any kind of predators in your home.

The difficult part is that African Spurred Tortoises are usually extremely vulnerable when they are domesticated. So, they become easy prey for animals like coyotes and foxes or even bobcats and raccoons. With animals like the coyote, you can even expect attacks in broad daylight. So you must take several preventive measures to ensure that your African Spurred Tortoises are safe.

Temporary fencing

Temporary fencing serves two purposes. It can be used to separate various farm animals and can also be used to direct them into their enclosures. The primary function of a temporary or portable fence is to mark boundaries and actually control your animal groups.

The most common type of temporary fence is the chain link fence. You can get long rolls of chain links that are arranged in a zigzag pattern. The heavy base allows you to place them where you need to. Another simple type of temporary fencing is the mesh fence. It is similar to the chain link fence but is more secure as the base is heavier.

For larger animals like the African Spurred Tortoise, you can also use a picket fence. They have vertically arranged wires that have a very strong base to keep these animals safe.

If you have poultry in your home, you can use chicken wires or poultry fences to keep African Spurred Tortoises and chickens separate. These fences are ready to install and can be adjusted as per your needs. They do not require any tools for installation and work perfectly well on all terrains.

Permanent fencing

Permanent fences do not serve the purpose of separating different farm animals. They are used to mark the boundary of your garden to prevent animals from getting out or getting in to your property. For instance, if you have a freeway near your home, a permanent fence will keep your African Spurred Tortoises from getting away from your garden or farm. They also keep predators at bay.

Needless to say, these structures, once installed, must not be removed. They must also be able to keep small animals and birds from getting in and out. In addition to that, they must also be strong enough to hold on for several years.

The most common type of permanent fencing used to keep your African Spurred Tortoises safe is the wooden or bamboo fencing. Panels of wood and bamboo are installed around the perimeter of your space. You must make sure that there are no gaps in between panels. Concrete fences are also used. They are sturdier and are also great at keeping predators away.

Electric fences are not the best. There are chances that your own pets will get electrocuted. Of course, it is a cruel option whether you are thinking of keeping pets in their boundaries.

Best fencing options

Proper fencing is necessary in order to keep your tortoises from entering any unsafe area on your property or from walking out onto a busy street. It also ensures that your tortoises are safe from any predators.

You also need good fencing to manage grazing. You can control the area that your tortoise grazes in so that they only get access to good fodder. This can be done with the help of temporary fencing.

Permanent fences are usually used to mark the boundaries of your property.

Whether you are choosing temporary or permanent fencing, here are the options available:

- **Barbed wire fence:** This type of fence consists of several strands of horizontal wire that has barbs every 12cms. Do not use wires that have barbs placed closer as it can lead to injuries.

- **Woven wire fence:** This type of fence contains smooth steel wires that are woven with horizontal and vertical wires. This is one of the most widely used types of fencing. However it is expensive and may not be as useful as high tensile wires.

- **High tensile wires:** You can choose either electric or non-electric fencing. It is more elastic, is lighter and more effective.

- **Interior fencing:** This may include a temporary electric fence or may use a permanent fence that divides the area. This helps tortoises stay in one area without any conflict or territorial behavior.

It is common practice to use electric wires. But make sure that your tortoises are trained to recognize the electric fence before you introduce them into a pasture with this type of fencing.

You can start by using one strand of hot wire at very low voltage near the water sources. Even a mild current is enough for the tortoises to recognize an electric fence and make sure that they stay clear of it.

7. Accessories

You should make sure that your Sulcata plays with the right kind of toys. Cheap plastic materials that can have an adverse effect on the health of the Sulcata must be avoided. Similarly, toys that can be shredded or broken should also be avoided.

The Sulcata might accidentally swallow the small or shredded pieces. Make sure that the toys that you allow the pet to play with are of good quality. They should be safe for the Sulcata, and they should be impossible to swallow for him.

Your Sulcata could actually shock you with the kind of things it can get hurt from. For example, the plastic rolls of toilet paper can be very harmful for the Sulcata because he can get his head stuck in it.

You should make sure any such potentially dangerous things are out of the reach of the Sulcata. Keep the bin and plastic shells away from him because he might try to play with things that could be harmful for him. This might be very difficult for you in the beginning to look into areas and places that have hidden dangers for the pet.

But, you will definitely learn with time and experience. Things in the nursery should be pet-friendly. You should make sure there are no sharp edges that could hurt the animal. Also, make sure that the Sulcata can't climb on the furniture.

If your pet Sulcata swallows something toxic for him, you might not even get a chance to take him to the veterinarian and save him. The digestive system of the animal is such that blockages can happen easily and they can be very dangerous. There are many animals that lose their lives because of such blockages.

This makes it very important to look for areas of hidden dangers and keep the pet safe. The Sulcata will try to swallow anything it can. It will try to swallow rubber items, though such things are very harmful for him. It is you who needs to make sure that the pet does not chew on the wrong items.

While they might like chewing on them, these materials when ingested will cause blockage of the digestive tract. You have to take measures to avoid such incidents in your home.

Hiding places

Sulcatas love hiding places. In their natural habitat, they have many hiding places. It is important that you provide the same when they are in captivity in your place.

A Sulcata loves a hiding place. They will use this place to hide, rejuvenate and rest. You can create small hiding places in the nursery of the Sulcata.

It is important that you use only safe materials to create the hiding places. You can make use of rocks and pipes to create such spaces. It is also important that you don't leave anything hanging.

Safety of the Sulcata is your duty. It is important to make sure that the Sulcata is not hurt by the hiding place or any other thing in the nursery. Make sure that there is nothing that can prick the Sulcata.

Many people prefer using a large number of rocks in the water nursery. This allows them to create many small hiding places. The benefit of these hiding areas is that the bacteria on the rocks are beneficial for the Sulcata.

It is important to understand the importance of hiding spaces for the Sulcatas. There are some people who keep only one or two rocks in the nursery. They believe that the Sulcata should be visible to them all the time.

Another suggestion that you can use while constructing the nursery is to make caves of different sizes for the Sulcata. This will help the Sulcata as it grows in size and dimensions.

You should make caves in a way that the Sulcata finds it easier to crawl inside them. There should be small holes that will help the Sulcata to peer outside from those holes in the caves.

It is important that the Sulcata is safe and sound. He needs to feel secure. Even if he is visible to you all the time, he might feel distressed and insecure. This is not right for the overall growth of the pet.

It is important that the pet is stress free. He should feel safe and secure. Hiding places will help him feel so. So, it is important that you provide many hiding places for your Sulcata in the nursery.

8. Heater

While you are setting up your nursery for the Sulcata, you might also have to place a heater inside the nursery. This will help to regulate the temperature in the nursery.

It should be noted that the place you reside in will affect the need of a heater. It is important that you understand the weather conditions in your area before you make a choice regarding the heater.

The choice of Sulcata will also affect the choice of a heater. You should understand that different species of tortoises have different requirements, even in terms of temperature.

In most cases, a heater and thermostat are used in combination in the nursery. This particular combination is required to keep the right and also constant temperature.

You will also need a thermometer to monitor the temperature. It is important that the thermometer is accurate. You should also take into account the size of the nursery when you are finalizing a heater.

You should get a thermometer installed inside the nursery of the animal. It is important that you check the thermometer regularly and make sure that the temperature is being maintained.

There are some people who install heaters for their entire home. But, this is not a very good idea because it will cost more and you will have to bear temperature ranges that you might not want to.

You can look at installing ceramic heat emitters or space emitters. It is important that the heater is installed perfectly so that there are no fire related incidents.

If you are planning on using heat pads to keep the pet warm then you should know that a heat pad can keep the thing that it is in contact with it warm, but it can't heat the air and water.

When we are talking about maintaining a consistent temperature for the pet Sulcata, we are essentially talking about maintaining the temperature of the place. The place needs to warm and be maintained at a certain temperature.

You can use a heat pad for extra warmth if needed. If your pet is not well or if you are trying to take him out of hibernation, you can keep the heat pad under the bed of the pet.

The heat pad will provide extra warmth to the pet and will help him to heal faster. But, don't rely on a heat pad to keep the temperature of the cage consistent.

You should be careful when you have heaters installed in your home or in the nursery of the pet Sulcata. Your smoke alarms should be in good condition. You should also make sure that the Sulcata can't get to the heat source. These all are precautions that you should take.

Space heater

There are many kinds of space heaters available on the market. You have the option of oil based space heaters or infrared heaters. These heaters are portable and easy to handle.

Space heaters are very easy to install. They come with a thermostat. The heater needs to be plugged in to the socket and the desired temperature needs to be set.

In comparison to a CHE, they are more expensive. The old models were not very safe, but the newer ones come with auto shut option, which makes them quite safe.

Ceramic heat emitter or CHE

A ceramic heat emitter is another popular choice of owners to give their Sulcatas a consistent temperature range. The CHE looks like a light bulb.

You can easily fix it like a light bulb. It is like a bulb that emits no light but generates heat. You will also have to purchase a CHE lamp to plug the emitter and a thermostat to regulate the temperature.

You can easily buy a CHE online. It is an excellent choice for heating the nursery of the pet animal, though it might not be suitable if you want to heat a room.

9. Lighting

This section will help you to understand the lighting pattern that needs to be maintained for the African Spurred Tortoise.

Artificial light

While you can't control when the sun rises and sets, you can provide adequate artificial light in the nursery of the pet. This will ensure that the pet gets consistent lights.

Some owners think that it is enough to make sure that the Sulcata is exposed to constant temperature. They believe that light cycle is not a crucial thing for a Sulcata.

You should know that this is absolutely false. If you don't expose your animal to consistent light cycles, he will try to hibernate, and in the process put himself into danger.

You can make use of desk lamp, reptile lamp or normal room light. You don't need a special kind of light. It just needs to be some light source.

You can manually switch the light on and off at approximately the same time to make sure that a consistent cycle is maintained. The problem with this system is that there is a chance of you forgetting to switch the light on.

A simpler way to take care of the light cycles is to set a timer. You can set it for a time period of twelve to fourteen hours. This system is more efficient and less troublesome for you.

Chapter 6: Diet requirements of the Sulcata

As the owner or as the prospective owner of a Sulcata, it should be your foremost concern to provide adequate and proper nutrition to the pet. If the pet animal is deficient in any nutrient, he will develop various deficiencies and acquire many diseases.

When the nutrition is right, you can easily ward off many dangerous diseases. Each animal species is different.

Just because certain kinds of foods are good for your pet dog, it does not mean that they will be good for other pets also.

It is important to learn about all the foods that the pet animal is naturally inclined towards. You should always be looking at maintaining good health of your pet.

It is important to learn about the foods that are good for your pet. But, you should also understand that the foods that you feed your pet with could be lacking in certain nutrients. An animal in the wild is different from one in captivity. Availability of certain foods will also affect the diet of your pet.

Generally, the food given to captive pets is lacking in certain nutrients. It is not able to provide the pet with all the necessary nutrients.

In such a case, you will have to give commercial pellets to your pet. These pellets are known to compensate for the various nutritional deficiencies that the animal might have due to malnutrition.

You should always aim at providing wholesome nutrition to your pet. It is important to understand the pet's nutritional requirements and include all the nutrients in his daily meals. To meet his nutritional requirements, you might also have to give him certain supplements.

The supplements will help you to make up for the essential nutrients that are not found in his daily meals. Though these supplements are easily available, you should definitely consult a veterinarian before you give your pet any kind of supplements.

It is very important that you serve only high quality food to your pet. If you are trying to save some money by buying cheaper, low quality alternatives, then you are in a bad situation. A low quality food will affect the health of the pet.

You can expect him to acquire deficiencies and diseases if he is not fed good quality food. The cure for this is taking the pet to the veterinarian. This in turn will only cost you more money.

To avoid this endless loop, it is better to work on the basics. Keep the pet healthy by feeding him with high quality foods, rather than spending money on him by taking him to the veterinarian.

The diet of the Sulcata will have a direct effect on the way he feels and functions. You should make sure that the staple diet of the pet is able to provide him with all the necessary nutrients.

The Sulcata will also enjoy the treats that you serve him. Maintain a good balance between the staple items and treats. You can choose from various food items to provide wholesome nutrition to the pet.

If you are unable to provide the pet Sulcata the food that he normally survives then he would not be able to survive well. So, it is better not to replicate the diet of other pets.

You can expect him to acquire deficiencies and diseases when he is not fed good quality food. The cure to this is scheduling appointments with the veterinarian. This in turn will only cost you more money.

Keep the pet healthy by feeding him with high quality foods, rather than spending money on him by taking him to the veterinarian.

1. The nutritional requirement of the Sulcata

People still don't know much about the nutritional requirement of the Sulcata. There are lots of studies and research that is still being done to understand the nutritional requirement of the Sulcata.

Many researchers are still researching the ideal diet of the Sulcata. Some believe that keeping the diet simple and close to the diet of a wild Sulcata is good for the animal.

The animal is mostly a herbivore. It is only during extreme conditions that the African Spurred Tortoise eats the animals taking refuge in its burrows.

The African Spurred Tortoise requires more fibre. The animal does not need too much protein in its diet.

It is important that you don't experiment with the diet of the pet animal. You can't feed him anything that you wish to. This is not good for the health of the pet.

If you are expecting that your pet Sulcata can live on a diet that a pet dog lives on, you are only making things difficult for the pet Sulcata. You will regret this later, so better to be careful for the Sulcata.

You should try to provide certain staples in the everyday food of the Sulcata. These staples are grass, leaves and vegetables. You should also make sure that the food that you choose to serve is of good quality.

The owners have the choice of feeding various commercial foods to the pet tortoise. It is important to check all the ingredients of commercial foods to be sure that the food is safe for the pet Sulcata.

You should never go by the brand picture to buy your pet's food. It is important to check the main ingredients and percentage of each ingredient.

It is better if the main ingredient of these foods is meat. You should avoid any food that has by-products of animals instead of the real food. You should also avoid food with ingredients such as BHT, BHA and ethoxyquin.

When you are buying food, you should also look for the ideal size. The pet Sulcata might not be able to eat a bigger size, and might even choke in it.

You can look for simpler shapes and sizes rather than fancy ones. If the size of the pieces is small, they are easier to eat and swallow, which is ideal for the pet Sulcata.

You should also make sure that the percentage content of each nutrient is just right for the Sulcata. It has been discovered that less protein in the diet of the pet can lead to various diseases and disorders.

The percentage of fat in the diet of the pet Sulcata will depend on the individual needs of your pet. If your pet Sulcata looks sluggish, you might want to lower the fat in his diet.

If you are looking to feed your pet Sulcata a simple yet good diet then you can go for commercial food along with some occasional fruits as treat. These treats will provide the necessary fibre in the diet of the pet.

Leafy vegetables are also considered to be highly nutritious for the pet Sulcata. It is believed that it is better than many other foods, but if the food pieces are bigger, it can be difficult for the pet Sulcata.

An ideal pet Sulcata diet would consist of up 25-30 percent of fibre, 10-15 percent of fat, 40 percent of carbohydrates, 10-15 percent of protein and minimum of 2 percent of vitamins and minerals.

Various oils also help to keep the fat content optimal in the diet of the Sulcata.

The carbohydrate in the diet is supplemented by grains, vegetables and fruits. On the other hand, the fibre in the diet is supplemented by grains, insects, vegetables and fruits.

To meet his nutritional requirements, you might also have to give him certain supplements. The supplements will help you to make up for the essential nutrients that are not found in his daily meals.

Though these supplements are easily available, you should definitely consult a veterinarian before you give your Sulcata any kind of supplements.

You also have the option of giving commercial food to your pet animal. But, it should be noted that no such food is complete in its nutritional requirement.

It is often believed that most commercial Sulcata foods are only equivalent to low quality food in their nutritional content.

This is not good for the pet animal's overall development. They contain big pieces of food, which are difficult for the pet animal to take in.

2. Food requirements of the Sulcata

As discussed in the previous section, you can look at including good quality grass and leaves or commercial food as the main food of the pet Sulcata.

There has always been a debate about the right food for the pet Sulcata. The pet Sulcata's diet is not so different from the wild one that it is all the more important to understand it well.

It is always recommended that the everyday diet of the pet Sulcata is closely worked out with a vet. This will help you to provide optimal nutrition to the pet animal.

You can also save yourself from making some big blunders. It is not a good idea to goof up a pet's diet in the name of experimenting.

You have to be sure before you can serve a food item to the pet. It is better that you spend some time in understanding the food requirements of the pet Sulcata. This will allow you to do the best for him.

The requirements of the Sulcata will change as he grows in age. The requirements will vary based on the age and also health of the animal.

If you find it cumbersome to cut food into small sizes, you can cut a big batch and freeze it. You can also look for places that offer small sized food for the pet.

You should aim at providing all the necessary nutrients to the pe through his food. In such a case, you can avoid giving any extra supplements to the pet animal.

At times, your pet's diet might not be able to provide it with the right set of nutrients and vitamins. In such a case, avoid administering any medicines on your own.

It is always better to consult a veterinarian before you administer any supplement to the Sulcata. You should also discuss the dosage with the veterinarian.

If the pet is not well and is recuperating from an injury or disease, the veterinarian might advise you to administer certain supplements to the pet. These supplements will help the pet to heal faster and get back on his feet sooner.

You should also make sure that the treat foods also provide some nutrition to the animal. While you can be sure that your pet is getting the right nutrients, the pet can enjoy the treat given to him.

You can also include supplements of fatty acids in the diet of the pet. A few drops of this kind of supplement will enhance the taste and the nutritional value of the food item that is being served to the pet animal.

While it can be necessary to supplement certain vitamins and nutrients to the pet, you should also be aware of the hazards of over feeding a certain nutrient.

If there is an overdose of a certain vitamin in the body of the animal, it can lead to vitamin toxicity.

You might even see that your pet is enjoying all the treats, but this in no way means that you can give him an overdose. You should always do what is right for the health of the Sulcata.

You can choose to serve clams to a pet animal, but it is not necessary. If the pet is being served high quality nutritional food, he can do without the clams.

The main benefit of adding clams in the pet's diet is that they will add a lot of fibre and protein in the pet's diet. Eating clams also gives the pet the mental stimulation of being in his natural habitat.

If you decide to feed clams to the Sulcata, then you should look for small sized clams. They should also be cleaned properly. These animals are safe and healthy for the pet animal.

Make sure that the food that you serve is not dirty or unhealthy. Such food items aren't very hygienic because of their poor sanitary conditions. Such a feed will only make the pet sick.

It is important to know where the food comes from. If you are oblivious about such things, you can never control what goes in the nursery.

Your lax attitude can make your pet sick. You have to make sure that the food is disease free before you feed it to the pet Sulcata.

The only way to ensure that healthy food is being served to the pet is to know where the food is coming from. It is better to spend some extra money and get good quality food than to compromise on the health of the pet.

3. How much to feed the Sulcata?

As a pet parent, you will have a hard time wondering as to how much food you should feed your pet animal. You don't want to over feed.

And, at the same time you don't want to leave him hungry. This can be tricky for any pet parent.

It is important that enough emphasis is laid on this particular point. If you are thinking that you need to feed the Sulcata three to four times a day, then you are wrong. The Sulcata does not need so much food.

The ideal scenario for the Sulcata is if you serve him good quality grass and leafy vegetables once a day for six days a week. Many people don't give food to the Sulcata for one day in the week. This helps the Sulcata to stay healthy and digest his food well.

Essentially, tortoises are anatomically designed to consume grass or roughage. Grain feeding involves providing tortoises with a certain ration that consists of a mix of different grains.

For a balanced meal, it is a good idea to allow the animals to graze at least once a day and then provide them with a grain mix or hay and alfalfa grass.

While nutritionally, grass feeding and grain feeding will not have too much difference, the latter makes the tortoises stressed as it is far removed from their normal biological need.

Therefore, a mix or adding supplements to grazing tortoises is recommended.

Grass

If you live in an area where there are significant non-grazing seasons, hay or grass can become the main source of nutrients for your tortoises. Hay or alfalfa provides the tortoises with protein and a good dose of energy.

Alfalfa is called legume hay and is more beneficial to your tortoise's health. In addition to high amounts of protein, they also contain calcium, vitamins and other minerals.

You must provide your tortoises with specially stored and cured hay for the best results.

On average, a tortoise will require about 4 pounds of hay every day. You should either make it available all day or make sure that the tortoises are fed twice each day even when the tortoises are browsing.

You also get alfalfa pellets that you can mix with the grains. This makes it easy to store and also reduces wastage.

Chaffhaye

Chaffhaye is a great substitute for grass hay. You can use early grass or alfalfa to make this. All you need is to chop the grass or alfalfa, spray with some molasses and add store bought culture of bacillus subtillis.

Then, you need to vacuum pack the mixture. This hay will ferment in the bag. The bacterial culture that you add aids digestion in tortoises.

This is a great source of minerals, vitamins and energy. On average, an adult tortoise will need about 2 pounds of chaffhaye for every 100 pounds in body weight. The nutritional value of 50 pounds of chaffhaye is equal to 100 pounds of high quality hay.

Grains

Pellet grain mixes, or grains, are great for your tortoise's diet. They provide minerals, vitamins and proteins. You can even give your tortoise store bought grain pellets that are formulated specially to provide nutrition to tortoises. These are the grain options that you can choose from:

Whole grain: this includes unprocessed seed heads of grains.

Pelleted grain: these products are made from whole grains or grain by-products that are broken into smaller pieces and then bound into pellets using a special agent.

Rolled grain: Rolled grain is similar to whole grain. It is different in shape and is flat because it has been rolled.

Texturized grain: This is similar to the previous option. The difference is that there are other ingredients that have been mixed with it to improve the health benefits.

Besides these regular foods, you must also provide your tortoises with supplements and medicated feed. This is extremely important if you are commercially rearing tortoises. You will also have to find good supplements if you have a pregnant doe or even an unwell tortoise at home.

Now, you can feed tortoises twice a day. Keep the feeding time consistent and make sure that there is a gap of 12 hours between each feed.

During the summers, appetite will decrease and it will help to provide the first feed earlier in the morning. You also must make sure that the tortoises are eating well. Ideally, the food that you provide should be consumed within 30 minutes, indicating a healthy eating habit.

4. Treats

You should also offer treats to the pet animal every now and then. It is important that the treats are healthy. They should not disturb the nutritional balance of the pet animal.

If you keep serving him the wrong kinds of treats, it will only affect his health in the long run. It is also important that the pet associates the treat with reward. He should know that he is being served the treat reward for a reason.

You will have to keep a check on the amount of treats a pet will get. This is important because treats are not food replacements. They are only small rewards.

You should always look for treats that are healthy for the pet. The pet should enjoy eating them, but their nutrition should not be compromised.

When you serve the treat, you need to make sure that you don't add any extra salt or sugar. Also, make sure that you cut the food item into small pieces. It will be easier for the Sulcata to eat it.

It should be noted that just because your pet animal seems to enjoy a treat, you can't give the food item to him all day long. You will have to keep a check on the amount of treats a Sulcata will get. This is important because treats are not food replacements.

If you keep serving him the wrong kinds of treats, it will only affect his health in the long run. The pet can suffer from diarrhoea and other disorders and problems because of consuming wrong food items. This is the last thing that you would want as a parent of the pet.

This section will help you understand various kinds of treats that you can serve your pet. The best kind of treat for a pet Sulcata is a food item that has meat as its main component. Sulcatas will love it, and it is also healthy for them.

Fresh scallops can serve as a very good treat for the pet Sulcata. It is good for the pet and is also delicious for him. It is important that only healthy items are served as treat items.

Corn chips are excellent for the withers because of the high saltiness. This makes them drink more water, preventing chances of calculi in the urine.

Apples, watermelons, peaches, bananas, grapes and dried fruit are among the favourites of tortoises. Give them small pieces of these organic fruits to prevent choking.

Vegetables like carrots, lettuce, pumpkin, spinach and any greens work really well with the tortoises.

5. Supplements

The diet of the African Spurred Tortoise should be highly nutritious. If you make sure that the African Spurred Tortoise is getting all its necessary nutrients from the food itself, you can avoid the use of supplements.

At times, your African Spurred Tortoise's diet might not be able to provide it with the right set of nutrients and vitamins. In such a case, it becomes necessary to introduce supplements in the diet of the African Spurred Tortoise.

If the pet is not well and is recuperating from an injury or disease, the veterinarian might advise you to add certain supplements to the pet's diet. These supplements will help the pet to heal faster and get back on his feet sooner.

You should always consult a veterinarian before you give any supplement to the African Spurred Tortoise. He will be the best judge of which supplements the African Spurred Tortoise requires and which ones he doesn't.

There are many vitamin supplements that are available in tasty treat forms for the African Spurred Tortoise. While you can be sure that your pet is getting the right nutrients, the pet can enjoy the treat given to him.

You can also include supplements of fatty acids in the diet of the African Spurred Tortoise. A few drops of this kind of supplement will enhance the taste and the nutritional value of the food item that is being served to the African Spurred Tortoise.

While it can be necessary to supplement certain vitamins and nutrients to the pet, you should also be aware of the hazards of over-feeding a certain nutrient. If there is an overdose of a certain vitamin in the body of the African Spurred Tortoise, it can lead to vitamin toxicity.

Another point that you should take care of is that you should not blindly follow the instructions and dosage that is printed on various supplements. The food that you feed the African Spurred Tortoise will also have a supply of vitamins. The African Spurred Tortoise will only require some extra dosage.

Avoid supplements that are labelled "African Spurred Tortoise minerals". These are always low in copper. It is better to use horse minerals or regular cattle minerals instead.

6. Foods that should be avoided

There are certain food items that should be avoided for the Sulcata. This section will help you understand these food items.

Keep the food simple and healthy. If you are giving fish, then you should make sure that it does not have bones because the bones can get stuck.

Your pet wouldn't know that these foods are not good for him. You should take it upon yourself to keep such foods away from the pet.

If you are looking for a comprehensive list of food items that are unhealthy for the pet Sulcata, then the given list will help you. You should try to avoid these food items:

- **Gold fish**: If you are serving fish as the main source of food for the pet Sulcata, you should remember that it is best to avoid gold fish. It is important that you avoid this food type in any form whatsoever.

- **Feeder fish**: The same goes for feeder fish as for gold fish.

- **Artemia or brine shrimp**: This kind of food item is not an ideal source of protein. It is advised to avoid it while you are deciding on food items for the pet Sulcata. Many young Sulcatas have shown severe consequences after consuming this kind of food item.

- **Sweeteners**: It is important to avoid corn syrup and sugar coated food.

- **Artificial preservatives**: They will add nothing to the diet of the pet. And, they are not good in the long run.

- **By products**: You should always try to give the pet the real thing. There is no need to serve by products.

- **Caffeine**: Sometimes, the children of the house can force the pet to consume such food items just for some fun. So, it is important that you keep a check on what the kids are doing when they are with the Sulcata. Make sure they do not feed him caffeine.

- **Citrus fruits**: Citrus fruits such as lemons, pineapple, oranges and limes are not suitable for a pet Sulcata.

- **Chocolates**: Chocolates are unhealthy for these animals. You should make sure that you keep these food items away from your Sulcata.

- **Raisins and grapes**: Grapes and raisins are toxic for the pet. If these food items are given for a longer duration, substantial damage is done to his health.

- **Peanuts:** Another food item that is dangerous for the pet is peanuts. Other legumes should also not be given to the pet animal. They can cause choking and vomiting.

- **Foods high in salt**: You should try not to feed foods that are very rich in salt content. You should keep all human junk food such as salted chips and nuts away from the pet Sulcata.

Chapter 7: Taking care of the Sulcata's health

It is important that you take care of your pet's health. The pet will depend on you for most of its needs. It will not be able to tell you if it is facing any discomfort regarding its health. You should be able to identify the symptoms of various diseases in your pet to treat it well.

If you take care of the diet of the pet, you can save him from many deadly diseases. You should make sure that the pet lives in a healthy environment. These simple things will help you to keep the pet healthy and fit.

You should also be able to diagnose any symptoms of injuries in your pet. If you can treat him in your home, then you should do it very carefully. In case you have any doubts, you should take the pet to the vet.

Maintaining the health of the Sulcata would always be your primary concern as the owner. The food that you give him, his environment, his hygiene levels, everything will ultimately affect his health conditions.

This chapter will help you to understand simple ways to keep the Sulcata healthy. You will also learn about the common health problems that can affect your Sulcata.

You should always make sure that your pet Sulcata is always kept in a clean environment. A neat and clean environment will help you to keep off many common ailments and diseases.

You should understand the various health related issues that your pet can suffer from. This knowledge will help you to get the right treatment at the right time.

It is also important that you understand how you can take care of a sick pet. This knowledge will help you to keep calm and help the sick animal in the best way possible. Proper care will help him to get better faster.

1. When should you see the veterinarian?

If you find your pet behaving different from normal, then the first step you should take is to provide him warmth. It is important that the pet is not cold and proper temperature is maintained.

Even after that if you see him deteriorating, it is time to see the veterinarian. If the condition is not very severe, you can book an appointment in the next three to four days.

But if there is an emergency, you should not waste time and should take the Sulcata to the veterinarian as soon as possible. You can also take him to the emergency clinic in your locality.

It is important that you are able to identify the signs of emergency in your pet so that you can act without delay. If you happen to notice the following in your pet Sulcata, you should know that it is an emergency and the veterinarian needs to be consulted:

- **Lethargy**: If the pet is not moving at all, try to increase the heat for him. If the pet remains to be unresponsive even after that, this can be serious. Don't do something drastic such as putting a stick in the bed. Just take him to the doctor.

- **Diarrhoea**: If the problem of diarrhoea or green stools persists for more than two days, you will have to get a faecal exam done for any complications. After you have domesticated a Sulcata for a while, you will be able to identify normal faeces and loose faeces.

- **Blood**: Blood from an arm or a small cut is not a thing to worry about. But, blood from urine is a cause for serious concern. It can get critical if not treated on time.

- **Vomit**: You might be surprised to learn that Sulcatas can vomit like many other animals. Any undigested food is immediately vomited. Vomit caused by poisoning, choking or sickness should not be ignored at any cost. You should be able to identify the vomit of the Sulcata so that you can take action.

- If you see the pet gasping for breath, or if you notice twitching or abnormal movements of limbs, you should consult the veterinarian as soon as possible.

Though it is always advised to take the pet to the vet if any health problem arises, it is always a great idea to keep a first aid kit ready. This will help in the case of minor injuries and also emergencies when you can't reach the vet.

The main aim of first aid is to give the pet some relief from his pain. Giving first aid would not be very difficult if you follow the right steps in the right order.

While you are giving the animal some first aid, there are a few things that you should do. This will help you to calm the Sulcata and also give him the necessary aid.

You should make sure that you don't aggravate the pain and misery of the poor animal in any way. You should follow the given procedures in the given order to help the Sulcata.

You should make sure that the airway of the animal is not blocked. Make sure that the Sulcata is able to breathe properly.

After you have made sure that the animal is breathing properly, it is important to check if he is bleeding. If the animal is bleeding, you should take the necessary steps to stop his bleeding.

You should also be able to examine how profusely he is bleeding. After you have succeeded in reducing the bleeding of the Sulcata, you have to take the necessary steps to maintain the right temperature of the pet animal.

If the body temperature is not maintained, it will worsen the condition of the pet. You should understand that the pet Sulcata is easily prone to stress. Injury and pain are two factors that can stress him a lot.

So, it is important that you take the necessary steps to reduce his stress levels. This might seem like an impossible and daunting task, but if you take the right steps, you will be able to calm your animal successfully.

When you keep a first aid kit, it is important that you have knowledge about each item. You should know how to use things. You should also replace stuff when they reach their expiration date.

The various items that the first aid box of the Sulcata should have are bottled water, hand warmers, paper towels, flash light, toilet paper scissors, tweezers, cotton swabs, hydrogen peroxide, saline water Neosporin and ensure.

When you are giving first aid to your pet, you should check their body temperature. They should neither be too hot or too cold. The tortoises need to maintain a warm body temperature at all times. When they are stressed or injured, it is all the more important for them to maintain a warm body temperature.

Tortoises have a lower body temperature when compared to the body temperature of the human beings. You should check the temperature of the animal. If he is hypothermic, you should make arrangements to keep him warm from the outside.

You should make sure that the pet is not overheated. Too much heat is not good for your pet. It can disrupt many normal functions of the Sulcata. If the pet is overheated, make sure that you cool him down.

This step becomes all the more important when you are dealing with tortoises. They will be unable to regulate their temperature. So, when you provide them with first aid, you will have to regulate their body temperature.

2. Maintaining records

It is advised to maintain regular health records for your pet. This will help you to understand his health in a better way. You would be able to detect even the smallest of issues with the help of these records.

For example, if you have a record of his size, you can notice any changes in the pet's weight. A drastic change in weight is often understood as an early symptom for diseases.

The pet can be saved from future health issues by keeping a simple record. If you can't keep a daily record, aim at a weekly record.

Record all the important parameters at the beginning of each week and compare with the previous week.

The parameters that you should be aiming to record are the weight of the pet, the physical activity of the pet and the food intake of the pet.

You can calculate the quantity of food that the pet consumes by counting the number of kibble or by weighing the food that you serve and then the food that is left.

You can record the physical activity by observing and estimating the time. You should also look out for any gunk formation or lump formation on the body of the pet. You should also make sure that there are no trappings of hair around the limbs of the pet.

A lethargic pet that shows no interest in movement is not a good sign. You will only know these things if you observe. If you notice any change in the pet's normal activity levels or weight, you should be alerted.

This definitely means that something is wrong with the pet. An early action can save you from many health problems in the pet. This is good both for you and the pet.

3. Diagnosing injuries in the Sulcata

Sulcatas, like the other tortoises, lead a very active lifestyle. They like moving around. Your pet is likely to spend most of its time doing so. This makes it susceptible to injuries.

There is nothing to worry about if your pet injures itself. You should be able to diagnose the injuries so that they can be treated well. You might even have to call the doctor from the doctor's clinic.

It is important that you learn the basics of diagnosing the injuries. This is important because if a small injury is treated well, the animal can be saved from a major problem in the future.

It is important that you understand that your pet animal might not show any signs of injuries, even when it is injured. It will be your responsibility to diagnose the injury before it turns into a bigger problem.

Looking for the symptoms of injuries

You should be on the lookout for any symptoms that your Sulcata might display when it is injured. These symptoms could mean that there is something wrong with your Sulcata. You should look carefully for the following symptoms:

- Is your Sulcata looking very disturbed? This could be because he is in pain.
- Is your pet looking very lazy and lethargic? This could be because he has injured himself and is in pain.
- The limbs of the animal could also be hanging. This is also a clear sign of injury to the pet. You should closely examine his limbs to be sure.
- Is your pet stumbling? Is the pet showing uncoordinated movements?
- The pet could be having frequent or infrequent fits.
- If there is a change in the way he carries himself, then this could also mean that the injury has forced the pet to change the way he usually is.
- The head of the pet could be hanging.
- You should look out for the faeces of the animal. If there is any change in the colour of the faeces, this could mean that there is something wrong with his health.
- Do you spot any blood on the skin of the animal? You should look for blood stains in the enclosure of the animal also. This could mean that something is not right.
- Look for certain common symptoms, such as coughing and vomiting by the animal.
- Do you witness any changes in the skin of the pet? If yes, then this could also mean that there is something that needs your attention.
- If your pet looks scared and tensed, you should understand that it is for a reason. You need to closely examine him to find out what is wrong.

When you spot any of the given symptoms in your pet, you should know that something is not right. You will have to take a closer look at the pet and examine. This examination will help you to understand if there is something wrong with your pet.

While you are examining your pet, you should also understand that your pet could be scared. It is important that you make the pet feel comfortable. This will help you conduct the examination properly and without any problems.

To make sure that the pet animal is not terrified when you are trying to examine him for any potential injuries, you can do the following:

You should make sure that you conduct the examination in a closed area, a place where the animal feels safe and protected. You should try to examine him indoors.

Do not let the place be crowded when the examination is being conducted. Make sure that all the other pets and your family members are outside and not in the same place where the examination is being conducted.

The noise level around you should be as low as possible. The noise will stress the pet and will irritate him, so make sure there is no noise around. Conduct the examination in a quiet place.

Be as gentle and kind as possible. This will help your pet to relax and feel less stressed. You should in no way add to the stress and pain of the pet.

If the animal will see you being fidgety, it will only add to his stress. You should be as calm and as confident as possible. Your confidence will give him some hope and relief.

Make sure that all the tools that are needed for the examination are ready. You shouldn't leave your pet alone to fetch the tools. Everything should be ready before the examination.

You should check his entire body. Remember to check on both sides of the body. Start the examination at one particular point and then move ahead from that point. The examination should be definite and guided and not random.

Look at how your pet responds to the body examination being done. If you feel that the animal is not taking it too well, you should stop the examination. You should look for any stress signs that he displays.

You should not ignore them; otherwise the animal can go into deep shock.

4. Stress in Sulcatas

If the Sulcata does not get proper heat and light, he can go into stress mode. His senses start to shut down. It should be noted that hibernation is not good for pet Sulcatas.

When the surroundings get very cold for the pet and the daylight shortens, the Sulcata's body starts reacting differently. This is not natural for them.

After years and years of captivity, the Sulcatas have also changed. They are dependent on consistent warm temperature for their well-being. Their bodies are not suitable to bear extremely cold weather or extremely hot weather.

When there is a decrease in temperature or change in light cycles, the Sulcata will panic. But, the body will give up very soon.

If too much time is lost, the Sulcata will not be able to come out of the state. You can even lose your Sulcata. As the owner of the Sulcata, it is important that you make sure that your pet does not go into this state. If this happens, things can get very complicated.

Your primary focus should be that the Sulcata remains healthy. This can be done by maintaining warm temperatures around the Sulcata.

You should make sure that there is a light cycle that is consistently maintained in the nursery of the pet. The area should also be at a consistent warm temperature.

You should also make an attempt to understand the signs of stress. If you see your pet going into that zone, you can make temperature and light changes in his surroundings to bring him back to normal. If you could touch the stomach area of the pet, it will be cold. The pet might also act very unusual. These are warning signals that the pet is getting stressed and shouldn't be ignored at all.

The first thing that you should do after encountering such warning signals is to warm the Sulcata. You should not increase the temperature all of a sudden. Do it gradually and consistently.

If you increase the temperature all of a sudden, the pet might go into a shock state. You can use a heater to warm the nursery, but the heater will need a lot of regulation so that it does not get too hot.

If the pet does not respond for a very long time, it is advised that you call the veterinarian to your home. The immune system of the pet will also suffer when he is trying to recuperate. You should extra care of him.

Make sure he is away from anything that can make him sick. You should keep an eye on the pet and lookout for signals.

A simpler way to avoid the pet to get stressed again is to keep the temperature of the nursery a few degrees more than what is normal for the Sulcata.

Signs of stress

There are a few symptoms that will help you to identify stress in your pet. You should stop the body examination as soon as you spot any of these symptoms. The following signs will help you to identify stress:

- The pet will try to escape you when it is stressed. It will not let you come closer to him and will get irritated.
- The pet will show violent movements. For example, the pet will strongly thump his tail on the glass of the nursery.
- The animal will show a drastic change in its activity level. There are a few animals that will get extremely active, while others will become very lethargic. They will not move at all.
- The pet would be seen grinding its body parts tightly and also flicking them.
- The pet would be seen shaking his head angrily. You would be able to make out that something is wrong with the pet.
- He would make strange and loud noises from his mouth, when not grinding his teeth tightly.

- If you measure the body temperature of the animal, there will be a change in the body temperature.
- The animal could also hurt himself. He might claw at himself.
- The Sulcata can eat its own arms when it is in stress. This is a self-cannibalism. It is very common in many species of Sulcatas.
- The animal would lick his various body parts, such as legs and feet.
- The young ones would show the symptom of diarrhoea. They will suffer from frequent and liquid stools.
- If the animal is not treated on time, you will see that his appetite decreases with time. It will decrease to a point that it will become difficult for the animal to carry on his daily tasks.

Reducing stress

At this juncture, you would want to reduce the amount of stress that your Sulcata is through. It is important that you take all the necessary steps to make the Sulcata feel safe and secure.

- If your pet is still very young, then you should keep his nursery in a secure and closed area. This will fill him with warmth. This is like a reassurance to the animal that he can be safe and secure.

- You should make sure that your pet can rest well in a calm environment. Keep him away from any place of commotion.

- Make sure that there are no noises around the animal. Any kind of noise will disrupt him and will agitate him.

- You should also try your best to make sure that there are no sudden noises around the Sulcata. The animal should be able to rest in a calm environment. Sudden noises and voices will disturb the pet and will agitate him further. It should be made certain that all the noises are eliminated.

5. Taking care of a senior Sulcata

A Sulcata of age four or five is said to be an elderly or senior Sulcata. It is important to care for the pet as he grows old. He will show certain changes in his body and behaviour that you should be okay with.

It is not right to expect a senior Sulcata to have the same energy levels as a younger one. The senior pet will exercise less, eat less and litter less. They will start becoming oblivious of their routine light schedule.

The pet will also show a decline in his capacity and eyesight. The pet will become lethargic. He will not have much energy and would prefer sleeping most of the time. He might want to spend most of his time hiding in the cage.

The Sulcata will also be stressed easily. Please don't force an elderly tortoise to act young. You have to let him be if you wish to see him happy. It is important that you don't keep unrealistic expectations from him.

There are a few things that you need to take care of. Make sure that the pet is not disturbed when he is hiding in one of the hiding places. You should be extra careful about the temperature of the place.

If you are using a heater, it is important to monitor it regularly. If the heater does not have an automatic shutdown, it can get too warm for the pet very quickly. This can be dangerous for the Sulcata.

If the pet is losing excessive weight, feed him with fat rich food items. You should also make sure that he not disturbed by children of the house. This can irritate the Sulcata.

Sometimes, children keep tapping on the glass of the nursery. This can irritate the Sulcata. You have to monitor the kids around the nursery. Your main aim should be to provide good food to the pet and let him rest well.

If the pet is experiencing any kinds of pain, you should consult the veterinarian. He might prescribe some pain relief medication. This will help the Sulcata to get some relief and rest. Never administer any drugs without consultation.

Though the pet will not show much inclination towards moving around, you should encourage him to do some everyday.

It is important that you maintain daily health records of the pet. The pet should be healthy even when he is four years old. Schedule frequent visits of the veterinarian and make sure that the Sulcata remains fit.

6. Common health problems of the Sulcata

An unhealthy pet can be a nightmare for any owner. The last thing that you would want is to see your pet lying down in pain. Many disease causing parasites dwell in unhygienic places and food.

If you take care of the hygiene and food of the Sulcata, there are many diseases that you can be averted. You should always consult a vet when you find any unusual traits and symptoms in the pet.

You should make sure that the Sulcata has all his food doses on time. Apart from this, you should take him for regular check-ups to the veterinarian. This is important so that even the smallest health issue can be tracked at an early stage.

At times, even after all the precautions that you take, the pet can get sick. It is always better to be well equipped so that you can help your pet.

A pet Sulcata is prone to certain diseases such as rotten skin and various infections. If proper care is not taken, you will find your pet getting sick very often. Another point that needs to be noted here is that you will have to be extra vigilant to understand that something is wrong with the pet.

This section will help you to understand the various diseases that a pet can suffer from. The various symptoms and causes are also discussed in detail. This will help you to recognize a symptom, which should have otherwise gone unnoticed.

Though the section helps you to understand the various common health problems of the Sulcata, it should be understood that a veterinarian should be consulted in case of any health related issue.

A veterinarian will physically examine the pet and suggest what is best for your pet animal

When you are looking to maintain the health of your pet Sulcata, then you should make an attempt to understand the common health issues that the animal faces. This will help you to prepare yourself well and also treat your pet well.

Understanding various diseases and their symptoms

Who wouldn't want their pets to be healthy? Nobody would want to see a helpless animal suffering from a disease. To make sure that your Sulcata enjoys good health at all times, it is important that you recognize the symptoms of diseases that can affect a Sulcata at an early stage.

If you can detect a disease in an early stage, there are more chances that the disease will be cured. To be able to do so, you should make an attempt to understand the various diseases that can affect a Sulcata along with their symptoms.

It is known that Sulcatas are not susceptible to diseases if they are given a good diet and given a good and clean environment. But, it is also known that Sulcatas are easily stressed.

They get insecure easily, which increases their stress. They are very sensitive to stress and you will have to make special efforts to keep the animal calm, safe and secure.

You should always make sure that your pet is always kept in a clean environment. A neat and clean environment will help you to keep off many common ailments and diseases.

There are some common health issues that your Sulcata is prone to, such as tumours and cysts. There are many issues that might not start as a big problem, but become serious problems if not treated on time.

You should also never ignore any symptom that you see because an ignored symptom will lead to serious problems later. As in humans, an early detected problem or disease can be treated easily in Sulcatas also.

The various diseases that your pet Sulcata can suffer from are as follows:

Tumours and cysts

Your pet is also at risk of various cysts and tumours. If you notice any bumps on the body of the Sulcata, don't take it lightly. This can be dangerous.

It occurs because of the uncontrolled growth of the cells in the Sulcata's body. Though this is very common in these animals, it can be difficult to detect, especially in the earlier stages.

It is known that older Sulcatas are more at risk of such tumours and cysts. But, various tumours can also attack younger Sulcatas.

You should never take any symptom lightly and should visit the veterinarian when you observe changes in a Sulcata. The veterinarian will conduct tests on the blood sample of the pet to confirm this health condition.

You can look out for the various common symptoms in the Sulcata to know that he is suffering from this particular disease. You will notice a sudden and drastic weight loss in the pet.

You will notice the pet to be very lazy and lethargic. It will appear that he has no energy to do anything. The pet will have visible bumps and changes in the skin texture. The pet will suffer from diarrhoea. The lymph nodes of the pet will also be swollen.

Another symptom that could accompany this disease is tiredness. The pet will experience some difficulty in his breathing and will acquire extreme tiredness.

Treatment:

It is important that you take the pet to the veterinarian. He will be able to administer certain medicines and injections. The veterinarian might also suggest surgery.

It is very difficult to save the pet after he has been diagnosed with a deadly tumour. Mostly, it gets detected in later stages, so the treatment becomes all the more difficult.

Because the symptoms of this disease are very general, it is suggested that you ask your veterinarian to conduct yearly tests for your pet.

This would help in detecting any issue in the very beginning, which makes it possible to treat it successfully.

Rotten skin

Sulcatas shed the skin around the arms frequently. This will cause small flakes or pieces to float in the water. If these pieces are not removed, it can lead to rotten skin. The skin of the Sulcata can also get infected by the bacteria on these skin pieces.

Sulcatas tend to suffer from the issue of dry skin many a times. Dry skin is categorised by flaky skin. Some people mistake it for an infestation of algae.

If you attempt to look through the glass of the nursery, you may see dry and loose flakes of skin. This is the main test of dry skin. There are a few causes that can lead to dry skin, such as improper diet and dry surroundings.

Treatment:

You can also use olive oil capsules or vitamin E oil. These oils are easily available in all health stores. You can also put two to three drops in his food or nursery.

Continuous use of good quality oil will show you excellent results in a few weeks. Pour two to three drops of the oil at least once a week in the nursery of the pet.

It is also highly advised that you buy a mist humidifier. This will keep the place warm and humidity up. When a Sulcata experiences low humidity levels, he can easily get dry skin.

If the problem does not end after all these measures, it is advised to get a skin scrape done by the veterinarian. This will help you to determine if there is more to the problem than what you understand.

Bacterial or fungal infection

Your Sulcata can also be infected by yeast, bacterial or fungal infections. This can be very lethal so proper care should be taken.

In case, you find the yeast infection symptoms, you should make it a point to take your pet to the vet. He will perform a stain test and confirm the presence or absence of the disease.

Causes:

There are many causes of the infection. The various causes that could be behind this health condition in your pet animal are as follows:

- One of the main causes of any infection in Sulcatas is lack of a healthy diet.

- If your animal is on oral antibiotics, then it will have some side effect on the body of the Sulcata. This infection could be one of the side effects of the oral antibiotics.

- Another common cause of this health condition in Sulcata is stress. When your pet animal is going through excessive stress, it will lead to this health condition.

- If there is poor hygiene around the Sulcata, it can also lead to this health condition or infection. You should try to maintain optimum hygiene levels at all times.

- If the Sulcata is suffering from some other infection or health condition, this infection could be a side effect of the health condition.

Symptoms:

There are certain symptoms that will help you to diagnose whether your Sulcata has a yeast infection or not. In case you find the yeast infection symptoms, you should make it a point to take your pet to the vet. He will perform a gram stain test and confirm the presence or absence of the disease.

The following symptoms will help you to confirm whether your pet Sulcata is suffering from this yeast infection:

- Do you smell something foul near your pet? If the answer is yes, then this could be the yeast infection.

- One of the early symptoms of this disease includes diarrhoea. If your pet is suffering from diarrhoea that you are not able to control, then your pet could be infected by this health condition.

- You should keep a check on the stools of the Sulcata. The colour and texture of the stools will help you determine whether the Sulcata has or not.

- Does your Sulcata suffer from frothy stools? Is the stool dark yellow or green in colour? If yes, then this could be a clear case of the yeast infection, thrush.

- As the disease progresses, you will see more symptoms resurface. The mouth of the Sulcata can get very sore and dry.

- Another symptom that you will notice as the disease spreads is lesions. You should be on the lookout for this particular disease.

Treatment:

If your Sulcata is suffering from thrush, you don't need to worry as it can be treated. It is advised to administer 0.1ml dose of antibiotic per one kilogram weight of the Sulcata. Nilstat will effectively treat this yeast infection.

This is the dosage that is generally advised to treat most infections. You can even consult your veterinary before you give the dose to your pet.

When you are providing the treatment, there are certain precautions you need to take.

- After administering medicine, the pet might suffer from diarrhoea for a few days. This state can typically last for 2-3 days. Make sure that you take care of the pet's diet during this time because that will help him to revive from diarrhoea.

- The best way to administer medicine to the Sulcata is to give each dose in between his feeds. This is the best way to help him fight against the diarrhoea.

- Another point that needs to be remembered is that you should never give the dose of medicine with the food that you serve the Sulcata. There are many people who dissolve the dose in the water itself. This is not the right way because this will kill all the nutrition. The Sulcata's health will only be harmed if you do something like this.

7. Senescence

It should be noted that a Sulcata has no fat reserve. The Sulcata can convert muscle to energy. During senescence body weight drops to almost half.

When you spot any of the given symptoms in your pet, you should know that something is not right. You will have to take a closer look at the pet and examine. This examination will help you to understand if there is something wrong with your pet.

While you are examining your pet, you should also understand that your pet could be scared. It is important that you make the pet feel comfortable. This will help you conduct the examination properly and without any problems.

You should make sure that you conduct the examination in a closed area, a place where the animal feels safe and protected. You should try to examine him indoors.

Do not let the place be crowded when the examination is being conducted. Make sure that all the other pets and your family members are outside and not in the same place where the examination is being conducted.

The noise level around you should be as low as possible. The noise will stress the pet and will irritate him, so make sure there is no noise around. Conduct the examination in a quiet place.

Be as gentle and kind as possible. This will help your pet to relax and feel less stressed. You should in no way add to the stress and pain of the pet.

If the animal sees you being fidgety, it will only add to his stress. You should be as calm and as confident as possible. Your confidence will give him some hope and relief.

Make sure that all the tools that are needed for the examination are ready. You shouldn't leave your pet alone to fetch the tools. Everything should be ready before the examination.

You should check his entire body. Remember to check on both sides of the body. Start the examination at one particular point and then move ahead from that point. The examination should be definite and guided and not random.

Look at how your pet responds to the body examination being done. If you feel that the animal is not taking it too well, you should stop the examination. You should look for any stress signs that he displays. You should not ignore them; otherwise the animal can go into deep shock.

After administering medicine, the pet might suffer from diarrhoea for a few days. This state can typically last for 2-3 days. Make sure that you take care of the pet's diet during this time because that will help him to revive from diarrhoea.

The best way to administer medicine to the Sulcata is to give each dose in between his feeds. This is the best way to help him fight against the diarrhoea.

Another point that needs to be remembered is that you should never give the dose of medicine with the food that you serve the Sulcata.

There are many people who dissolve the dose in the water itself. This is not the right way because this will kill all the nutrition. The Sulcata's health will only be harmed if you do something like this.

8. Euthanasia

If you are still not aware of the procedure of euthanasia, then it is important that you understand the reasons that go behind euthanizing a Sulcata, or any other animal for that matter. It is important that you understand that no one conducts this procedure for fun.

Euthanasia can put most people in moral dilemma. There is always this question whether this is right or not. It is always advised that you should talk to vets and other pet parents before you can take a decision of your own.

You might have to take the decision to euthanize your pet Sulcata. It is important to understand that younger and smaller Sulcatas can be easily euthanized with the help of ethanol. You might have to carry out a more elaborate procedure for older and bigger Sulcatas.

Euthanasia has always been a subject of debate. Doctors all over the world are always debating whether euthanasia is morally right or not. This decision lies with you. But, you should understand that sometimes there is no better way to relieve your pet.

Reasons to euthanize your Sulcata

If you are still not aware of the procedure of euthanasia, then it is important that you understand the reasons that go behind euthanizing a Sulcata, or any other animal for that matter. It is important that you understand that no one conducts this procedure for fun.

Sometimes, there is no option left with the the vet except to euthanize the Sulcata. The following reasons are some of the major reasons that go behind euthanizing a Sulcata:

- **Health issues**: Bad health is generally one of the main reasons to conduct the procedure. Even if the pet is young, but very ill, the vet might euthanize him if there is no hope for his survival. In many such cases, the only way to relieve the Sulcata or any other animal is to conduct the procedure of euthanasia on him.

- **Old age**: Old age is also a very common reason to euthanize an animal. Once the Sulcata is old and incapable, it can get very difficult for him. If the vet feels that the pet's condition is only deteriorating, he might take the decision to conduct the procedure.

- **Lethargy**: Lethargy due to illness or age is a reason to euthanize. If the animal has become so lethargic that he can't go through most of his routine things, it can be very difficult for both the animal and the pet owner. In many such cases, the only way to relieve the Sulcata or any other animal is to conduct the procedure of euthanasia on him.

Mechanisms of Euthanasia

It is important to understand euthanasia properly so that you don't have any doubts about the mechanism. Many a times, confusion of certain techniques leads to many misconceptions. You should try to save yourself from such misconceptions.

Debates that revolve around euthanasia also discuss whether the mechanisms involved in euthanasia are correct or not. Such debates have been going on for too long. Research all have different views.

It is advised that you learn about the various techniques and mechanisms involved. This knowledge will allow you to have a deeper understanding about this topic. You can understand what your Sulcata will go through if you opt for this technique.

When you are looking at ways to euthanize your old Sulcata, you will definitely be hounded by the questions as to what the various mechanisms of euthanasia are. This section will help you to understand these mechanisms.

Euthanizing agents cause death by three basic mechanisms:

- direct reduction or depression of the brain's neurons which are extremely critical for various life functions,

- hypoxia,

- the physical act of disruption of the entire brain activity.

The main aim of euthanasia is to eliminate pain, distress and anxiety before the loss of consciousness.

Conclusion

Thank you again for purchasing this book!

I hope this book was able to help you in understanding the various ways to domesticate and care for an African Spurred Tortoise or a Sulcata.

If you wish to raise a Sulcata as a pet, there are many things that you need to keep in mind. It can get very daunting for a new owner. Because of the lack of information, you will find yourself getting confused as to what should be done and what should be avoided. You might be confused and scared. But, there is no need to feel so confused. After you learn about the Sulcatas, you will know how adorable they are. You should equip yourself with the right knowledge.

If you are still contemplating whether you want to domesticate the Sulcata or not, then it becomes all the more important for you to understand everything regarding the pet very well. You can only make a wise decision when you are acquainted will all these and more. When you are planning to domesticate a Sulcata as a pet, you should lay special emphasis on learning about its behaviour, habitat requirements, diet requirements and common health issues.

The ways and strategies discussed in the book are meant to help you get acquainted with everything that you need to know about Sulcatas. You will be able to understand the unique antics of the animal. This will help you to decide whether the Sulcata is suitable to be your pet. The book teaches you simple ways that will help you to understand your pet. This will allow you to take care of your pet in a better way. You should be able to appreciate your pet and also care well for the animal with the help of the techniques discussed in this book.

Thank you and good luck!

References

Note: at the time of printing, all the websites below were working. As the internet changes rapidly, some sites might no longer be live when you read this book. That is, of course, out of our control.

https://www.tonmo.com

http://www.reptilesmagazine.com

https://pethelpful.com

https://www.lllreptile.com

http://www.tfhmagazine.com

https://en.wikipedia.org

https://www.lovethatpet.com

https://www.thespruce.com

https://www.bluecross.org.uk

http://www.drsfostersmith.com

https://www.cuteness.com

http://jacksonville.com

http://www.vetstreet.com

https://www.hillsborovet.com

www.training.ntwc.org

www.wildlifehealth.org

http://animaldiversity.org

https://www.yourpetspace.info

http://healthypets.mercola.com

https://www.petplace.com

CPSIA information can be obtained
at www.ICGtesting.com
Printed in the USA
FSHW021219050520
69872FS